Private Lessons

Private Lessons

Customized and Personalized Instruction Tailored to the Individual Golfer

BY THE EDITORS OF *GOLF MAGAZINE*

TRIUMPH
BOOKS
CHICAGO

Produced and distributed by Triumph Books.

This book is available in quantity at special discounts for your group or organization. For further information, contact:

Triumph Books
644 South Clark Street
Chicago, Illinois 60605
(312) 939-3330
Fax (312) 663-3557

Printed in the United States.

ISBN 1-57243-292-6

Book design by Eileen Engel.

Jacket design by Mike Mulligan.

CONTENTS

PRIVATE LESSONS

FOREWORD

Any golfer knows that a private lesson doesn't come cheaply. Along with the considerable time investment, most top-notch instructors charge hundreds of dollars to correct a swing, teach putting skills, or perfect a chip. Once the lesson is over, you leave with a few pointers, and—if you practice—the possibility that these pointers will make it into your game.

If you're like most golfers, though, that practice time won't be readily available and before you know it, the lesson will be lost. You could return to the instructor, review the techniques, and start over again. Of course, this is all at the cost of another lesson and even more time.

So there are private lessons. And then there are *Private Lessons*.

Like personal instructors, GOLF MAGAZINE also charges for its lessons—for the cost of a single issue, you can turn to the brown kraft-paper pages of our instructional feature, *Private Lessons*, to find a wealth of information aimed at improving your golf game.

Each month, *Private Lessons* offers sage instruction to golfers of all levels—power hitters, straight hitters, senior players, low handicappers, and high handicappers. These customized lessons offer invaluable tips on the physical and mechanical aspects of golf—the long game, short game, putting, and address—along with the things instructors don't often teach—the mental game, strategy, and shotmaking—to name a few.

Private Lessons: Customized and Personalized Instruction Tailored to the Individual Golfer provides a sampling of the lessons collected from ten years of *Private Lessons*. Arranged by subject, this book is a marvelous way for golfers of any age and any level to brush up on the fundamentals, work on troublesome areas, and shave a few strokes off that next round.

Best of all, you can return to these pages at any time to revisit a lesson learned or to improve another aspect of your game—one of the best golf bargains around.

This book may not use the brown paper, but it still offers the finest in golf instruction through the rich text and illustrations. Enjoy.

George Peper
Editor-in-Chief
GOLF MAGAZINE

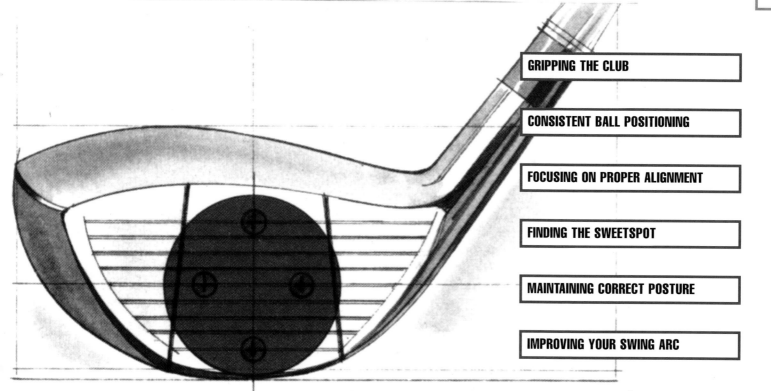

The Address

GRIPPING THE CLUB

CONSISTENT BALL POSITIONING

FOCUSING ON PROPER ALIGNMENT

FINDING THE SWEETSPOT

MAINTAINING CORRECT POSTURE

IMPROVING YOUR SWING ARC

GRIPPING THE CLUB

The importance of gripping the club in a comfortable and effective manner cannot be stressed enough. A good grip places the hands comfortably on the club and keeps them there securely throughout the swing so they function as a unit. If you aren't happy with the feel of the club in your hands or the success of your shots, a grip change might be the answer. There are three accepted grips—overlap (or Vardon, after Harry Vardon, the great British player who popularized it), interlock and 10-finger (or baseball). The instructions given here are for right-handers; left-handers should reverse everything. Whatever grip type you employ, remember always to start with the palms of your hands facing each other, with the back of your left hand facing the target.

THE OVERLAP

Probably the most popular grip today is the overlap. Take the club in your left hand as you normally would, then put your right hand on, overlapping the little finger of your right hand onto your left so it lies snugly in the valley formed between the index and third finger of your left hand. The ring finger on your right hand should butt firmly against the side of your left index finger.

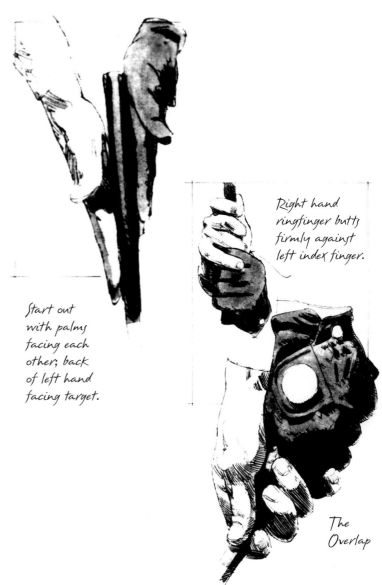

Start out with palms facing each other; back of left hand facing target.

Right hand ringfinger butts firmly against left index finger.

The Overlap

2

THE INTERLOCK

Golfers with small hands and short fingers might not feel they get a secure enough hold with the right hand using the overlapping grip. In that case, go to the interlock, which intertwines the little finger of the right hand with the index finger of the left, firmly meshing the hands. (Bear in mind, though, that the interlock isn't the prerogative of small-handed golfers. If the grip feels good and works well, use it.)

THE 10-FINGER

The 10-finger is the least common grip, but that shouldn't deter you from using it if it feels comfortable and secure. To take the 10-finger grip, simply put all 10 fingers on the club, butting the little finger of the right hand against the index finger of the left, the way you do when holding a baseball bat. Beginners usually hold the club with the "baseball" grip before graduating to either the overlap or interlock. If you like the baseball grip, stay with it. If you've never tried it, you may want to give it a shot, taking care to place the hands snugly together. ■

Little finger of right hand twines with index finger of left.

The Interlock

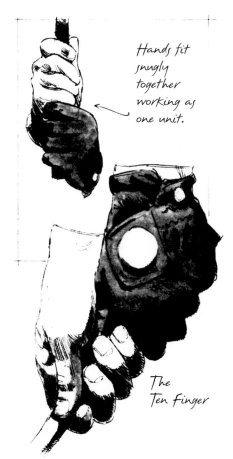

Hands fit snugly together working as one unit.

The Ten Finger

CONSISTENT BALL POSITIONING

If your set-up and swing were perfect, like a machine, you'd hit nothing but long, straight golf shots. But if you moved the ball out of position, you'd mishit everything, no matter how good your swing was. True, your swing isn't perfect, but ball position is still a vital ingredient in determining the quality of your golf shots.

SYMPTOMS

If you're hitting a lot of topped and thin shots, you're probably playing the ball too far forward in your stance. Weak hooks off the toe of the clubface indicate you're standing too far from the ball, and heeled shots to the right probably mean you're too close.

WOODS

When using a driver or a fairway wood off a tee, play the ball opposite your left heel to encourage a sweeping action that will give the ball plenty of air time. Tee the ball so that the top edge of your club is level with the middle of the ball. When your ball is on the ground, position your wood shots about one inch back from your left (front) heel. Without the advantage of the tee, you need to strike your woods with a slightly more descending blow to get them airborne.

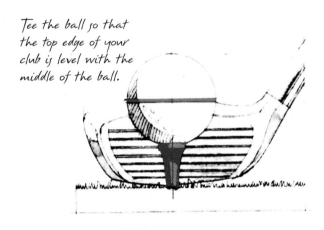

Tee the ball so that the top edge of your club is level with the middle of the ball.

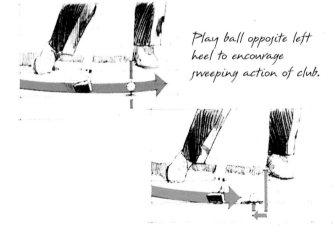

Play ball opposite left heel to encourage sweeping action of club.

Play ball one inch back from left heel for slightly more descending blow.

IRONS

Position your long irons the same as your fairway woods, one inch behind your left heel. Locate your mid- to short irons (5- to wedges) in the middle of your stance. This will insure that you hit your approach irons cleanly, imparting the backspin you need to keep your shots to the green on line and under control. Take care not to tee your ball too high with the irons. The ideal height allows you just enough clearance to slide the narrow end of a tee between the ball and the ground.

DISTANCE: A FIST PLUS A THUMB

Your clubs differ in length by half-inch increments, so to add consistency to ball positioning, use the following routine: Take your normal set up, soling the club behind the ball. Remove your right hand without changing the position of the club and make a fist with your thumb extended. Lay your fist against your left thigh and your thumb should just touch the butt of your club. ■

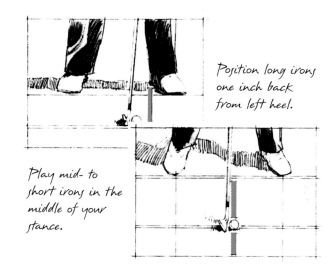

Position long irons one inch back from left heel.

Play mid- to short irons in the middle of your stance.

Right thumb touches butt of club.

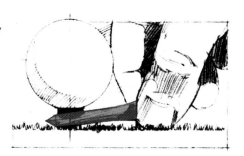

Determine the ideal ball height by sliding a tee between the ball and the ground.

FOCUSING ON PROPER ALIGNMENT

Faulty alignment can ruin your shot before you swing the club. Aiming the body somewhere other than parallel to the target makes a good swing bad and a bad swing worse. Examples:

1) A good player with a solid swing gets sloppy and starts aiming left of the target. He can't figure out why his shots tail-hook to the left, so he tries to prevent the clubface from releasing through impact and loses distance. Good swing gone bad.

2) A golfer who cuts across the ball from outside in and slices begins aiming right of the target to encourage an inside-out swing and a draw. He pulls the club inside the target line on the backswing, but then loops it over the top and cuts across the ball even more, resulting in a bigger slice. Bad swing becomes worse.

Learning to align yourself properly doesn't require physical skill or years of experience, just care. Here's how:

LEARN WHAT SQUARE IS

You may know that proper alignment means setting your feet, knees, hips, shoulders, and clubface square to the target line. But do you know what it feels like? Maybe not. It's very common for amateurs (and pros, too) to drift or twist themselves unknowingly into faulty alignment positions. That's

To recognize how square feels...

Take address position with feet parallel to club on ground.

If the club aligned with your knees, hips, etc., is parallel to the one on the ground, you are truly in a square position.

why it's crucial that your body recognizes how square feels.

Lay a club on the ground and stand with your feet shoulder-width apart, parallel to the shaft. Take another club and make an imaginary address position: knees flexed, bent forward slightly from the hips, back straight, arms hanging from shoulders. Without changing your body position, lay the club in your hands across your knees. Is it parallel to the

GOLF
MAGAZINE

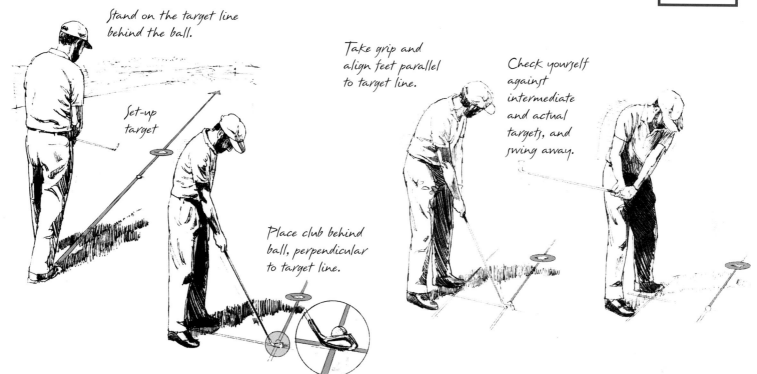

Stand on the target line behind the ball.

Set-up target

Place club behind ball, perpendicular to target line.

Take grip and align feet parallel to target line.

Check yourself against intermediate and actual targets, and swing away.

club on the ground? It should be. Do the same for your hips and shoulders; this will show if your body has a "feel" for setting up square.

REAL SHOTS

Good alignment starts with the clubface; get that square and the rest of your body will follow more easily. Begin by standing behind the ball, on a straight line with the target. To make squaring the clubface easier, pick a spot—a leaf, divot, whatever—that's on the target line and no more than

a couple feet in front of the ball. This is your target during the set-up.

Walk around and put the club behind the ball so the clubface is perpendicular to the target line, facing the intermediate spot you chose. Take your grip, then align your feet perpendicular to the clubface and parallel to the target line. Once your feet are square, your knees, hips, and shoulders should fall into place. Check yourself against the intermediate target and the actual target, then swing away. ■

FINDING THE SWEETSPOT

Nothing matches the feeling of hitting a ball squarely on the sweetspot on the tee shot. Not only does it feel good, it produces a good result—a long, powerful drive. Because this distance is often accompanied with accuracy, it's crucial that you learn to hit all your shots "on the screws." Here are a few tips that should help.

PROPER DISTANCE AT ADDRESS

You must stand the proper distance from the ball at address. Crowding or standing too far away from the ball produces weak mishits. To find the right spot, stand erect with your feet shoulder-width apart, flex your knees till the kneecaps are directly over each instep. Bend at the waist, keeping your spine straight and letting your arms dangle loosely until your fingertips are about three inches from your kneecaps. Bring your hands together on the club and waggle your body into a comfortable position. A correct and comfortable address position also helps maintain good balance throughout the swing: Falling toward the toes or heels during the swing is a major cause of "toed" and "heeled" shots.

Set up with the left arm straight and extended at address.

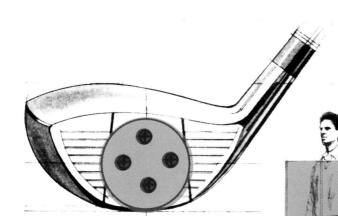

DRILL: Off the Screws

To improve your ability to hit the ball with the center of the clubface, practice intentionally making off-center contact. On the range, try to hit tee shots with the heel of your driver, then with the toe. Your feel for clubhead position through the hitting zone will increase, making it easier to make contact "on the screws." ∎

KEEP THE LEFT ARM EXTENDED

The left arm is the radius of your swing arc; if it bends, the clubhead moves. Therefore, you want the left arm in the same position at impact as it was at address. To assure this, start with the left arm straight at address and try to straighten it into impact. You can allow it to bend naturally on the backswing since centrifugal force will cause it to straighten naturally on the downswing.

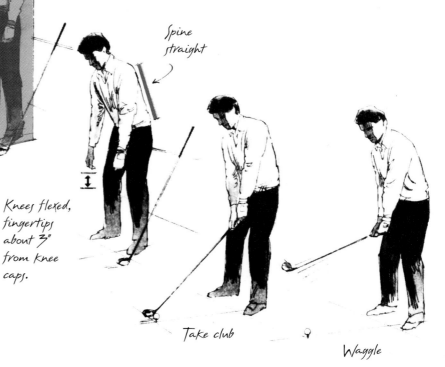

Spine straight

Feet shoulder-width

Knees flexed, fingertips about 3" from knee caps.

Take club

Waggle

MAINTAINING CORRECT POSTURE

To hit the ball long distances, you must use the large muscles of your back and hips. They are the body's prime source of power. In the middle of this power machine is the spine, holding it all together. To use the big muscles properly, it's vital that you can recognize and execute proper positioning of the spine throughout the swing. A look at a sequence of the swing shows that although your torso rotates, the angle of the spine remains constant until well into the follow-through. Here's what you need to know.

ADDRESS SETS IT ALL UP

Because it's easier to maintain good spinal position than create one during the swing, be sure you have it right at address. There are two angles to consider:

THE BEND

To achieve a proper spine angle at address, bend forward from the hips while keeping your spine as straight as possible. A straight spine tilts your torso forward so your arms hang freely from the shoulders. Bend until the hands are approximately six inches from the thighs. As you bend from the hips, don't lock your legs. Instead, maintain a slight flex in your knees. To make the most effective turn, your spine must be as straight as possible. Keep your chin up rather than dropping it toward your chest. If the chin drops, the top of the spine will curve.

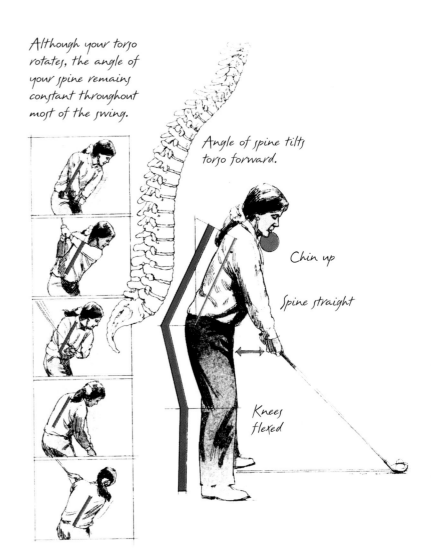

Although your torso rotates, the angle of your spine remains constant throughout most of the swing.

Angle of spine tilts torso forward.

Chin up

Spine straight

Knees flexed

THE TILT

You probably know that staying behind the ball is an essential part of hitting with power. You may not know that your ability to stay back is determined by your spine position from address to impact. Besides angling your spine toward the ball, you must also tilt it slightly away from the target. This keeps your head, shoulders, and sternum behind the ball so you can swing the clubhead on a level path into impact. To find the proper amount of spinal tilt, assume your normal stance (feet shoulder-width apart, knees slightly flexed, upper body bent forward from the hips). Hold your driver against your sternum so the clubhead is under your chin and the grip hangs between your legs. Without adjusting your legs, tilt your upper body to the right until the grip touches the inside of your left thigh. This puts your head, shoulders, and sternum in the proper position behind the ball. ■

Staying behind the ball at impact is essential to hitting with power.

This exercise will help you find the proper amount of spinal tilt.

Tilt upper body to right until grip touches inside of left thigh.

IMPROVING YOUR SWING ARC

Picking the club up with the hands in the takeaway is a sure-fire way to kill potential distance. It's not only difficult to return the hands to the proper position on the down-swing, but the arc is shortened, making it impossible to generate maximum clubhead speed. To create an arms-shoulder take-away and a wide arc, try hovering the club at address. Instead of resting the sole of the driver on the grass, hold it in the air, lining up the sweet spot right next to the ball. You'll feel a dramatic difference, as this transfers control of the club from your hands to your shoulders, making it easy to initiate a one-piece takeaway. Additionally, since there's no chance of dragging the club along the grass, you're guaranteed a slow, smooth swing. ■

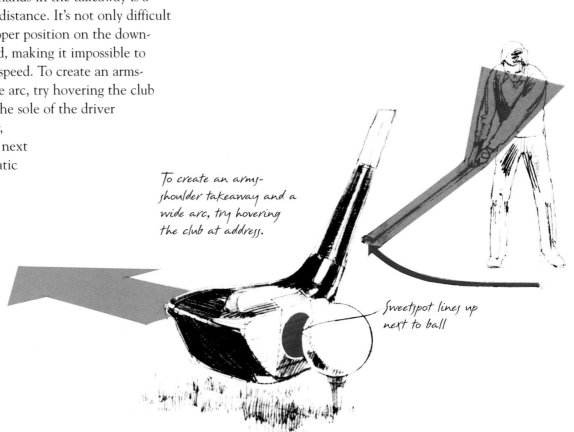

To create an arms-shoulder takeaway and a wide arc, try hovering the club at address.

Sweetspot lines up next to ball

The Full Swing

UNLOCKING THE WRISTS FOR POWER

SHAPING THE DOWNSWING

CONTROLLING YOUR HIPS

CONSISTENT PAR-3 WOODS

HOW TO: THE PHONE BOOTH SWING

HOW TO: THE 1-2-3 SWING

UNLOCKING THE WRISTS FOR POWER

Why do some golfers hit the ball much farther than others? Size, strength and agility play important roles. But few golfers can hit for good distance without uncocking the wrists through the impact zone. If you've made a full backswing turn and started down by shifting your weight onto the left foot, you've got the makings of a good release. Your legs and hips unwind your torso, followed by your shoulders, arms, wrists and hands. The "delayed hit" keeps the wrists cocked until the bottom of the downswing. There are two mistakes you can make: Releasing your wrists too early or not at all. Most golfers release their wrists too early, giving into the "hit impulse" at the start of the downswing. Instead of starting down with the legs, they initiate the downward action with their shoulders and arms, forcing the wrists to release while the club is still in the downswing. Distance is lost when you throw the club prematurely with your shoulders and arms. You can't "make" your wrists release at the perfect moment—the downswing happens too fast. But you can build the centrifugal force that makes it happen by starting the downswing with a shift of your lower body. "Frozen" wrists that never release usually result from mistrusting your swing and consciously blocking or steering the clubface and the ball toward the target.

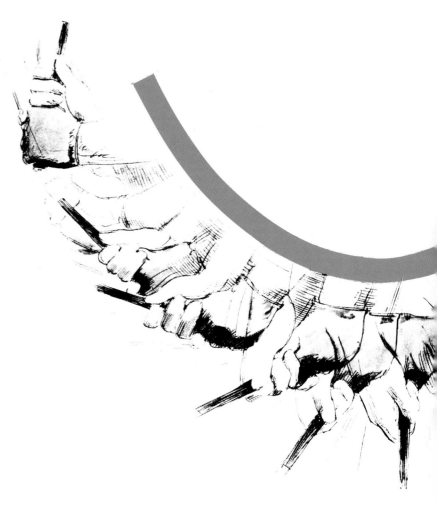

You may be hitting fairly accurate shots, but your club-to-ball contact feels wooden and lifeless and you're losing 20 to 30 yards on tee shots. Start your corrections on the practice tee. Loosen everything up, lighten your hold on the club and relax your entire body as you prepare to swing. After reaching the top and making your weight shift to the left foot, just let the shot go! When you begin doing this, your shots will fly farther—and probably to the left of the target as well. Expect it because you've probably been aligning your body well left of the target, giving the old no-wrist swing a chance to "block" the ball on line. Combine your new releasing swing with a square alignment and you'll be longer, straighter and more consistent. ■

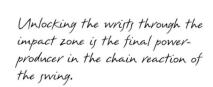

Unlocking the wrists through the impact zone is the final power-producer in the chain reaction of the swing.

SHAPING THE DOWNSWING

Most players know the backswing is important, but they should also realize that they can get away with some imperfection in that area. The downswing isn't as accommodating: At impact there is only one clubface angle and path that will produce the desired shot. Here are a few downswing thoughts that might work for you.

TRIGGER DOWNSWING WITH LEFT ANKLE

Solid contact and straight shots come from proper sequencing on the downswing, which means that it must start from the ground up. One way to start the downswing is to roll the left ankle toward the target. Think of this move as the first domino: The ankle moves the knee, which turns the hip, which turns the torso, which unwinds the shoulders, and swings the arms and club into the ball.

PUT YOUR FOOT DOWN

Some players get into a rut of errant shots—blocks or pull hooks—when their right hip becomes overactive and slides toward the target, pulling the club off-line. To quiet the right hip and get the club back on the proper path, focus on the right foot. Concentrate on keeping it flat on the ground during the downswing and past impact. Don't let it roll inward toward the left. Keeping it flat

Trigger your downswing by rolling your left ankle toward the target.

Concentrate on keeping your right foot flat during the downswing and through impact.

will keep the right knee slightly bowed out
and prevent the right hip from sliding through
too early.

SWING LEFT PAST THE BALL

A simple way to shape the downswing is by
working on the follow-through. Some players
tend to develop a swing path that is too far from
the inside, producing blocks and hard-to-control
hooks. If that's you, try this follow-through
thought: Focus on swinging the club left, or more
around your body on the follow-through, rather
than out toward the target. You may feel that
your swing will produce a huge slice, but in
reality, the low-and-around follow-through will
keep your club moving down the target line on
the downswing rather than inside out. A good
key is feeling as if your upper left arm stays mar-
ried to your chest until the last moment of the
follow-through. As your torso rotates through
the ball, your hands and the club will naturally
move left. ■

*Focus on swinging the club
left, or more around your
body on the follow through.*

CONTROLLING YOUR HIPS

One way to control your game is to control your hips. If the hips are too active—turning more than 45 degrees in the backswing—chances are your body is too active, which results in poor club control. The following hints will help you establish the right amount of hip action.

ARE YOUR HIPS TOO ACTIVE?

Instruction books that call for extra rotation of the hips are directed primarily at shorter hitters who can build more power with a bigger lower-body coil. If distance is not your problem, it's likely you turn your hips too much in the backswing, leading to swaying, overswinging and other direction-destroying faults. Check your hip action by setting up square at address and placing a club across your toes. Swing your driver to the top and freeze your lower-body position. Lower the driver to parallel your hips, the shaft about two inches from your body, and note the angle formed between the driver and the club on the ground. An angle of more than 45 degrees means your hips are too active and your hip turn needs to be reduced. When you swing the club back, try to keep the right hip still. Don't worry, the hips will turn; but by consciously keeping the right hip stationary, you'll cut down the amount of lower body coil.

On the backswing, your hips should turn no more than 45 degrees.

45 degrees

DOWNSWING: SHIFT, DON'T SPIN

Another fault is opening the hips too quickly on the downswing, causing pulls and slices. If these shots are characteristic of your game, work on initiating the downswing with a shift of the hips toward the target rather than turning or spinning them. The lower body will still rotate correctly on the downswing, but not so hard and fast as to misguide the club's path into the ball. ■

Opening the hips too quickly on the downswing will cause directional problems.

Initiate the downswing by shifting the hips toward the target.

Compare the angle formed by the two clubs to determine if you have too much hip movement.

CONSISTENT PAR-3 WOODS

If you find yourself using woods for your tee shots on some par threes, you need a method to make these powerful wood shots hold the greens. When hitting anything from a driver to 5-wood, remember: They're not designed for a lot of backspin, like irons, so to make sure they fly high enough to land softly and stop quickly, a few adjustments in your address position are necessary. Start by teeing the ball up about a half-inch higher than you ordinarily would. Widen your stance about an inch with each foot for stability, and play the ball forward, off your left instep. These adjustments will put you in position to make impact as the club is traveling on a slight upswing. Make your normal swing and the ball should take the higher, softer trajectory necessary to hold the green. ■

When using a wood on a par three...

Tee ball up half-inch higher

Widen stance

Play ball forward

GOLF
MAGAZINE

FULL SWING **2**

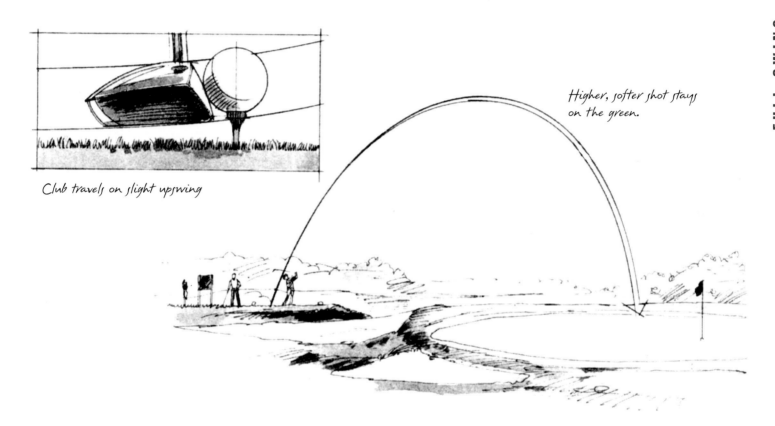

Higher, softer shot stays on the green.

Club travels on slight upswing

HOW TO: THE PHONE BOOTH SWING

Players who are good at keeping their shots in play usually have neat, compact swings free of excess motion. These golfers look as if they could tee it up in a phone booth. If you are plagued by control problems, try stealing a few secrets from the compact swing.

STANCE: NOT TOO WIDE

Players who take a big rip at the ball often set up with their feet very wide apart, which allows them to swing hard without losing balance. Your feet should be no wider apart for the driver than just outside shoulder-width. If you can't maintain balance with the feet in this position, either you're swinging too hard or your weight distribution at address is poor. (Weight should be evenly divided between the left and right foot and balanced on the balls of the feet.)

Some guys have such a compact swing that it looks as if they could hit out of a phone booth.

Handkerchief

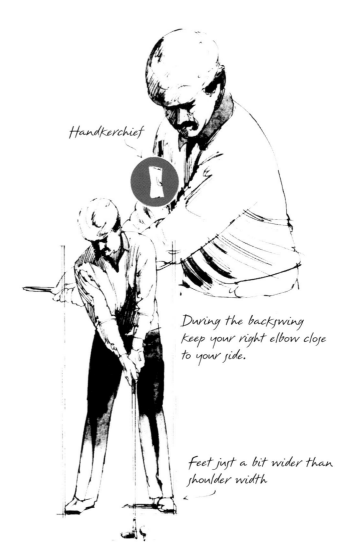

During the backswing keep your right elbow close to your side.

Feet just a bit wider than shoulder width

BACK: RIGHT ELBOW IN

To get into a compact position at the top, keep your right elbow close to your side on the backswing. An old trick is to tuck a handkerchief under your right armpit during the backswing; if your elbow moves too far from your side, the handkerchief falls free before the downswing starts.

TOP: WEIGHT INSIDE RIGHT

Most long hitters make a good weight shift, but even this is easily overdone. Sliding your weight to the outside of the right foot at the top may feel powerful, but it leads to a sway and poor impact. Your weight should move onto the inside of the right foot, not the outside.

DOWN: LEFT ELBOW IN

On the downswing, keep the left elbow close to your left side, which keeps the club moving on the proper inside-to-square downswing path. Allowing the left elbow to separate freely from your side usually results in an outside-in downswing and a pull or slice. If you make all the right moves, your arms will feel slightly restricted and your swing shorter. ■

You should feel as if your arms are tied and your swing is shorter.

Left elbow close to left side

Weight on right instep

HOW TO: THE 1-2-3 SWING

Many players get a thrill out of booming their shots, but chances are that their quest for power has made their swing rhythms erratic because they're swinging too hard. A rushed or poorly-timed motion eventually reduces power because it lessens the chance of making good clubface-to-ball contact. If you can keep your swing rhythm constant from takeaway through impact, you're more likely to stay in balance and deliver the clubface squarely to the ball. One of the tried-and-true ways of doing this is with the 1-2-3 swing.

USE YOUR OWN TEMPO

Everyone has an ideal tempo, not only for swinging a golf club but for any physical movement. So suggesting a count-system doesn't mean that every golfer should swing at the same pace. But within the individual swing, the sequence of motion should be smooth and even. If, for example, you lurch into the downswing from the top, this change in speed probably will throw you off balance and out of position. Here are the steps in the count:

Count "one" for a slow, even takeaway.

Count "two" to help you set the club at the top with a slight pause.

1) The Takeaway A slow, low takeaway, with the left arm pushing the club straight back with no wrist break, should be the first piece of your swing. The key is to start this move slowly: It's almost impossible to be too slow. Your one-count should cover the distance the club moves away from the ball until you feel your weight beginning to shift to the inside of your right leg.

2) Up to the Top The transition from backswing to downswing is a crucial step that most players rush. As you complete the backswing and set the club at the top, count "two." By counting a beat, you get a slight pause at the top of your swing. This pause ensures a smooth, uncoiling motion rather than a lurching action dominated by the right hand, arm and shoulder.

3) Through Impact Count "three" as you release the club through the impact zone. Your arm swing will continue down at the same pace as it did on the backswing.

Many power hitters (and would-be power hitters) think they must deliberately accelerate the arm swing through impact. That's unnecessary: The centrifugal force that's built up during the swing naturally increases the clubhead speed to its maximum at impact without your help. Say the three-count in the same relaxed tone as your "one" and "two." This counteracts the natural tendency to tense up through impact and lets your hands release the clubhead smoothly and freely. Try the 1-2-3 method as a means of maintaining a smooth swing rhythm from start to finish. When you hit the ball squarely, you'll gain both accuracy and distance. ∎

"Three" keeps your arms moving at a constant rate through impact.

3

The Short Game

EMPLOYING SIMPLE WEDGE TECHNIQUES

DEVELOPING A ONE-SWING CHIP SYSTEM

DELICATE FRINGE PLAY

CRISPER CHIPS AND PITCHES

FEELING THE CLUB

EMPLOYING SIMPLE WEDGE TECHNIQUES

Some players who could lower their score by sharpening their short game technique too often are scared of the wedges. Laying the blade of a pitching or sand wedge behind the ball conjures up thoughts of chili-dips, skulled shots and worse. In rushing to get the shot over, they rush the swing as well, virtually guaranteeing a poor shot. If wedges scare you, here's a three-step process to simplify your short game and start bringing down your scores.

1) KEEP THINGS SIMPLE

You've probably seen pros on television opening their stance, laying the club wide open and making other changes in technique to hit finesse shots. But you should stop experimenting and go with the basics. Keep things as simple as possible by using your normal grip and a square clubface. Open your stance only slightly. After you start making consistently crisp contact you can experiment with stance, grip and clubface alignment to play different shots.

Feel the clubhead as it moves back and through.

Grip lightly

Envision a rollercoaster as it negotiates a large dip...

It starts down slowly...

Gradually accelerates smoothly through the bottom of the arc...

Then slows down again as it climbs upwards.

3) SLOW AND SMOOTH

A major cause of mishit wedge shots is excessive body movement, usually caused by swinging too quickly. If the body lifts during the downswing, the clubhead hits high on the ball, causing a bladed or skulled shot. If the body drops, the club hits behind the ball for a fat shot. A hurried downswing also may cause coming over the top and pulling the ball left.

Think of the wedge as a precision instrument used to hit the ball an exact distance and direction. The wedge should be handled lightly, with deftness and finesse, not heavy-handedly. Hold the grip lightly and take half-swings without thinking about mechanics. Concentrate solely on feeling the rhythm of the clubhead back and through. Envision a roller-coaster as it negotiates a large dip: Starting downhill slowly, it gradually picks up speed and accelerates through the bottom arc, gradually slowing as it climbs the next hill. Forget about the ball and try only to swing the clubhead with that same rhythm. ■

SHORT GAME **3**

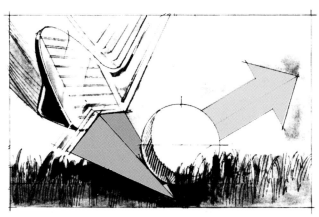

To get the shot in the air, drive an imaginary wedge of wood underneath the ball with the leading edge of the club face.

2) HIT DOWN FOR UP

Don't try to scoop the ball in the air by exaggerating hand action. The ball doesn't need help—that's the reason the clubface is angled. To let the club do its job, you have to hit down on the ball. Force yourself to hit down by imagining a small wedge of wood behind the ball. Aim to drive the wedge under the ball with the leading edge of the club, and you'll get the ball airborne while eliminating blades and skulls.

DEVELOPING A ONE-SWING CHIP SYSTEM

When you're trying to get the ball close from just off the green—inside a five-foot circle around the hole—line isn't as important as distance. You'll have an easier time controlling the distance if you use the same swing and different clubs (with different amounts of loft) to provide the amount of carry and roll necessary.

This one-swing system makes shot execution as simple as possible. When setting up, start with your weight leaning forward, toward the target, and play the ball well back, off your right ankle. Use an arm-and-shoulder stroke to take the clubhead back approximately two feet and come down through the ball, swinging the club at least two feet past impact. This stroke creates the same amount of force every time, because gravity does most of the work on the downswing. For longer or shorter shots, use a less- or more-lofted club. The obvious question: How do you choose what club to use? Keep it simple. Practice so you know how each club makes the ball react, then choose the club that will carry the ball three feet onto the green with enough speed to roll it into the hole. ■

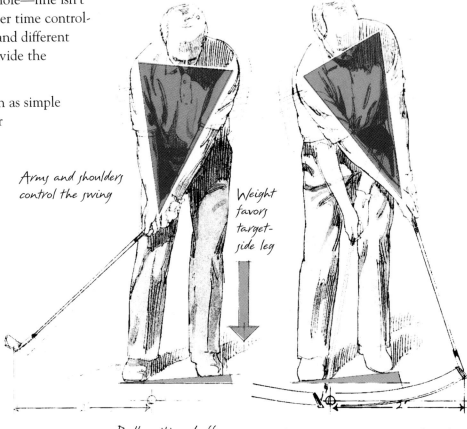

Arms and shoulders control the swing

Weight favors target-side leg

Ball positioned off right ankle

Follow through the same length as your backswing

Choose the club that will carry the ball three feet onto the green and with enough speed to roll it to the hole.

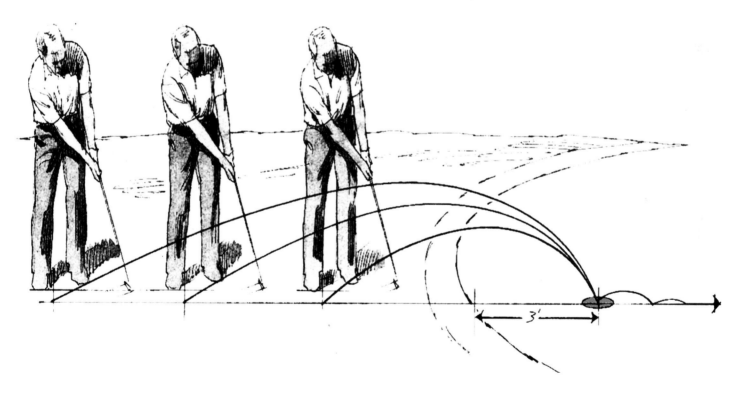

DELICATE FRINGE PLAY

A big part of becoming a good golfer is learning to make strong choices when faced with a variety of options on the course. A perfect example is when your ball comes to rest on the fringe of the green. Should you chip the ball or putt it? Whichever you choose, if you're not completely sure you're doing the right thing, your effort will be tentative at best. It's important, then, to know all the pros and cons involved when there's a choice to be made.

GENERALLY, GO TO THE PUTTER

Most golfers have better control over their putts than their chips, so it makes sense to putt the ball whenever the situation allows. Because the fringe grass is longer than the grass on the green, you'll have to hit the ball a little harder, which is something you'll get a feel for over time. You may find it helpful to play the ball forward in your stance to catch it slightly on the upswing. This will pop it into the air just a hair, like a mini-chip, and give it some overspin. Work on this technique on the practice green.

WHEN NOT TO PUTT

Putting from the fringe becomes ill-advised if the fringe grass is wet or unusually thick, or if the fringe slopes upward and your ball lies below the level of the green. In these cases, the smart play is a chip shot. Choose a club that's lofted enough to pop the ball over the fringe but gets it rolling on the

When deciding whether to chip or putt from the fringe, it's important to know the pros and cons.

Putt the ball whenever the situation allows.

Ball pops up like a mini-chip

Play ball forward in stance

green as soon as possible. Often you won't even have to use a real chipping stroke; you can just "putt" the ball with a short iron or wedge. Use your normal putting grip, holding the shaft vertically, so the heel is off the ground. Then make a simple arms-and-shoulders stroke.

WHEN NOT TO CHIP

Never chip from the fringe when the green slopes downhill to the hole, unless the hole is a long distance away, like 40 feet. On most downhill shots, you'll want to take advantage of the fringe, letting it slow the momentum of the ball so it trickles down to the hole. If you chip the ball and land it on the downslope, it kicks forward and is often difficult to stop near the hole. ■

Arms-and-shoulders stroke

Chip if the ball lies below the level of the green.

Hold the club vertically with the heel off the ground.

Use a putting stroke with a short iron or wedge, getting it rolling as soon as possible.

When going downhill, putt the ball through the fringe to slow it down.

SHORT GAME

3

CRISPER CHIPS AND PITCHES

If your shots regularly sail off-line between tee and green, it's to your advantage to be able to get the ball up and down. Some players have few problems hitting the ball solidly (though wildly) on full-swing shots, but sometimes they have trouble making solid contact with finesse shots—chips and pitches. The combination of an errant approach with a thinned or chili-dipped short shot is bound to produce at least a bogey, if not worse. The following tips may help you make crisper contact on chips and pitches.

DOWNWARD BLOW PREVENTS FAT SHOTS

Hitting a short shot fat (so it falls well short of your target) may be caused by several faults. One is trying to help the ball into the air by scooping under it. To get the ball airborne on a short shot you have to hit down on it with a descending blow, hitting the ball first and trusting the club's loft the same way you would with a full-force shot. First, be sure your set-up promotes striking the ball with a firm, downward blow. Your stance should be narrow (about three inches at the heels for chips; six inches for pitches), with the ball no farther forward than your left heel. Choke down on the shaft to increase clubhead control. Hands should be even with or slightly ahead of the ball—not behind it.

Hands even or slightly ahead of ball

Choke down on shaft

Narrow stance

Ball no farther forward than left heel

Focus attention on front of ball

GOLF
MAGAZINE

To ensure good balance stay crouched and keep your knees flexed through impact.

Finally, focus your attention on the front of the ball, not the back, and let the hands lead the clubhead through impact.

CROUCH MORE TO STOP THINNED SHOTS

A "thin" chip or pitch happens when the club's leading edge hits the ball just below its equator, causing the shot to fly lower and harder than normal. A thinned short shot comes from the same source as a thin full shot: The upper body rises as the club swings forward, lifting the downswing arc so the leading edge of the club strikes high on the ball. Rising on the shot usually is caused by standing too straight at address. Be sure to get into a good crouch, flexing your knees and bending well at the waist. Weight should be balanced between the feet as well as between the heels and balls of the feet. Imagine resting your chin on a shelf and keep it there—don't lift it—as you swing back and through. Also, be sure the ball lies between your left heel and the center of your stance and isn't too far back.

DRILL: Left Hand Only

Although the short shots require only short swings, you still need all the clubhead control you can get. To build control and feel, choke down and practice hitting chips and pitches using your left hand only. Hit a few shots, then use both hands again. Club control will feel much sharper and positive. ■

SHORT GAME

3

FEELING THE CLUB

The standard response to pitching and short wedge problems is to search for a mechanical stroke. However, in many situations, technique is rarely the problem with your wedge shots. Many times, it's an absence of touch, meaning your hands are not communicating what the club is doing to the rest of your body. In this case, the body takes over, with inconsistent results. A simple remedy at address can put the club back in control. As you address the ball for a pitch shot or short wedge, lift your hands so the club hovers about a half-inch above the ground, with the heel slightly higher than the toe. This puts your wrists in a slightly arched position, allowing you to feel the club's weight in your hands. You want to retain this feeling throughout the shot: The more you can feel the clubhead, the more it will swing itself, and the better the results will be. ■

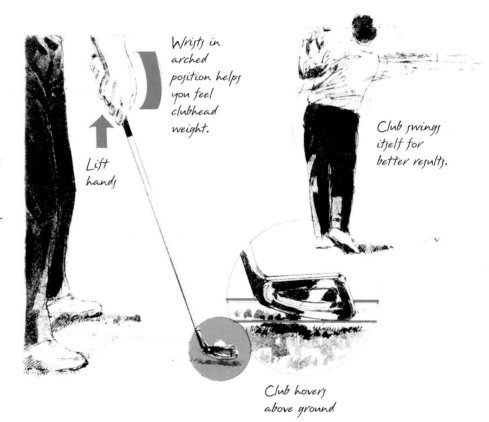

Lift hands

Wrists in arched position helps you feel clubhead weight.

Club swings itself for better results.

Club hovers above ground

Sand Play

SAND TRAP SET-UP AND EXECUTION

What's the worst mistake you can make in the sand? Leaving it in the bunker? No. The worst is hitting the ball before the sand and blading it over the green. You could find yourself in an unplayable lie, or worse, out of bounds. Here's a simple trick to ensure that you hit the sand first. Take the standard bunker shot set-up: feet pointed slightly left of target, ball forward in the stance, clubface slightly open. Then set your hands well behind the ball, so you feel a cupping in your left wrist. Pick up the club with your wrists to start the backswing and swing smoothly into the sand along the line of your feet. By using this very wristy stroke, where you set your hands at address is where your club will want to hit the lowest point of its arc. Setting your hands behind the ball is insurance against blading it. And don't worry about taking too much sand. You can hit up to five inches behind the ball and still escape if you make a full follow-through. ■

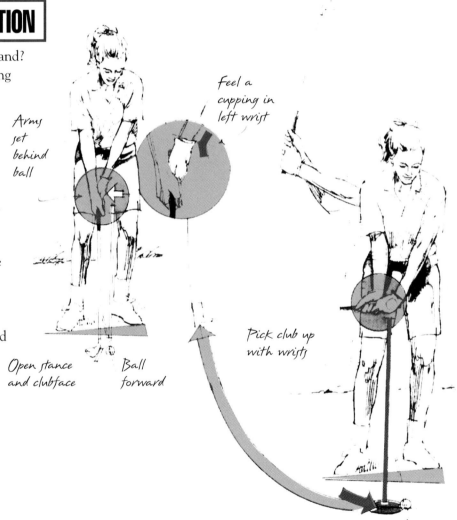

Arms set behind ball

Feel a cupping in left wrist

Open stance and clubface

Ball forward

Pick club up with wrists

Club will enter sand at lowest point of arc.

FINESSING YOUR SAND SHOTS

What's worse than hitting an approach shot into sand? Stepping into the bunker and flailing away with words like "dig," "blast," or "explode" in your head. The last thing you want is for sand shots to become an exercise in, well, exercise. With the proper technique, your basic sand shot can be just as smooth and relaxed as an easy half-wedge from the fairway. The key to easy-swinging sand shots is taking less sand. But rather than making contact closer to the ball, take a shallower angle of attack. One adjustment in your set-up should do the trick: Don't aim your feet so far to the left. Lay the face of your wedge open, so it points right of the target, and play the ball forward, opposite your front foot. Make a smooth swing along your stance line, holding the blade open through impact. Rather than exploding through the sand, you should feel as if you're "nipping" the ball off the surface. Done correctly, the ball will stop quickly after landing. ■

Take less sand and hold blade open through impact.

Open the clubface

Clubface points right of target

Slightly open stance

Ball forward

SAND PLAY

4

BEATING THE BURIED LIE

You're right where you don't want to be—in the bunker. If that weren't bad enough, the ball is plugged, most of it below the surface of the soft sand. Be confident; don't let the situation beat you before you make the shot. You may not be able to knock this shot stiff, but unless the ball's totally buried, you can get it out.

FORGET THE SAND WEDGE

From most bunker shots you'd use a sand wedge, which has a large flange that allows it to skim rather than dig through the sand. But for a buried lie you must dig deeper than normal so that the sand behind the ball pushes it up and out. The sand wedge won't dig deep enough no matter what you do. Instead, turn to the pitching wedge. Its smaller flange allows the leading edge to dig, and in most cases you can get it under the ball.

FORGET NORMAL TECHNIQUE

From a normal bunker lie, you address the ball with the blade of the sand wedge open to facilitate skimming and add loft to the shot. Also, you swing with an active right side, slapping or slicing through a thin layer of sand so the ball pops up softly and with backspin. This technique won't work on the buried lie. Here, you must address the ball with the face of the pitching wedge square or even

Address with both stance and clubface square, weight left and grip firm.

You must generate enough force to fly the ball to the green; let it run from there.

slightly hooded. Keep your stance square with the weight on your left side and the ball centered between your feet. Aim to hit the sand two inches behind the ball. Use a steep arm swing back and through, keeping the weight left. You should feel that the left arm and side are pulling the club down. The deeper the lie, the more you hood the blade and the harder your swing.

FORGET THE PIN

The ball will fly onto the green in a burst of sand. It will roll a long way after it hits because you can't put backspin on this shot. So, if the pin is cut close to the bunker, forget about getting the ball close. You want to hit the shot with enough force to carry the bank and hit the green. Then let it roll. With the pin toward the far side of the green, you can get it close simply by letting the ball run to the hole. ■

SAND PLAY

4

SAND SHOT #1: THE LONG EXPLOSION

At least once a round an approach shot will come up very short and finish in a bunker 20 yards or more from the pin. Often the ball has rolled into the trap, which means you'll have to fly over a wide expanse of sand before finding the green. The prospect of leaving the ball in the bunker makes this an unusually frightening shot.

LONG AND SLOW

A ball that has barely rolled into the trap should have a good lie. You can float the ball from the sand instead of popping it out. To do this, take a shallow cut of sand at impact. Set up with a closed stance and open the clubface slightly. Swing back using the same technique as for a short pitch and run. Keep the wrists firm and make a three-quarter backswing. Control the downswing with your arms and keep the club moving lower through the hitting area so that it skims the sand. The ball will carry the lip, land on the green halfway to the hole and roll the rest of the way. ∎

You will have to fly over a lot of sand before finding the green.

Closed stance

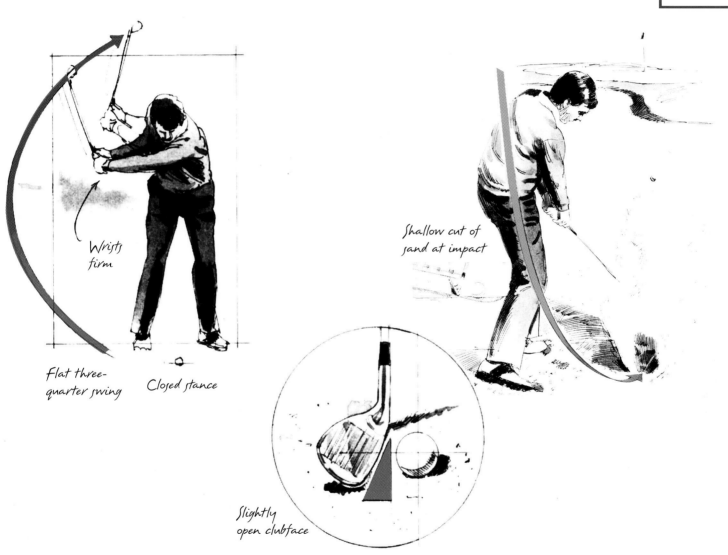

Wrists
firm

Flat three-
quarter swing

Closed stance

Shallow cut of
sand at impact

Slightly
open clubface

SAND SHOT #2: THE SHORT EXPLOSION

There is one shot from sand that can spook even the best of players: The short explosion. The situation is paradoxical: The ball lies a few yards from the hole, yet it's hard to put it close. Because the ball has to move a short distance, even good golfers shy away from swinging as firmly as they should. Instead, they decelerate on the downswing and leave the ball in the bunker. Or they get anxious and catch the ball clean, launching it well past the target. The key to playing the shot is to make a brisk swing without sending the ball too far. To do this, vary the club's point of entry into the sand: The farther behind the ball it hits, the more sand has to be moved and the shorter the shot. For example, you might want to take twice as much sand, so make contact three inches behind the ball instead of an inch and a half. Don't decelerate. Power the club into and through the sand to be sure of hitting the ball out of the trap. (The more sand you're planning to take, the more important it is to accelerate throughout the shot.) Another key to the short sand shot is a steep swing: The more abruptly you pick the club up, the higher and shorter the ball will fly and the more quickly it will stop on the green.

Quick wrist cock

Steep takeaway

Take twice as much sand as you would normally.

Power the club through the sand.

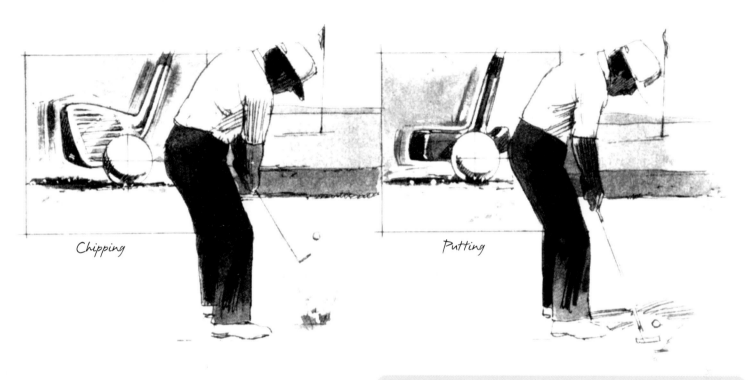

Chipping

Putting

OTHER OPTIONS

Under certain conditions, you may not have to chance the explosion at all. If there is little lip and the lie is clean and flat, you can chip the ball out. You also might try putting out, but only if there is no lip and the fringe is well trimmed.

DRILL: Shovel the Sand

To get used to taking and moving a lot of sand and getting a short result, hit balls from a practice bunker by taking three times as much sand as usual. (Draw a line behind the ball to mark entry point.) Soon you'll lose your fear of taking a big swing in order to hit a short explosion. ■

SAND SHOT #3: THE FLOP SAND SHOT

To threaten par, you must fire at the pin. When you're on target, the result is makable birdie putts; when you're slightly off, the ball often finds a bunker near enough to the pin that there's very little green between the ball and the hole. The common mistake is to shorten your swing and try to hit a soft, spinning shot. Unless your timing is perfect, you either skull the ball or leave it in the sand. The shot to play is a flop: a high-flying, soft-landing shot that stops almost immediately upon landing. And the vital ingredient for this shot is not unbelievable touch, but an understanding of the proper technique, which is not all that complicated.

Clubshaft bisects triangle

Clubface open and pointing to sky

VISUALIZE THE TRIANGLE

The key to the flop is the set-up. Once correctly over the ball, just swing naturally. To ensure a proper set-up, visualize a triangle: One side runs down the target line; a second runs through the ball and perpendicular to the target line; the third connects the two on your side of the ball at a 45-degree angle. At address, your stance should be so far open that your feet run along the third line and your right foot nearly touches the target line. Open the clubface so it is nearly perpendicular to the target line. As you address the ball, the clubshaft should bisect the triangle and the clubface should point to the sky. From here, swing along the line of your feet. Because the clubface is so open, the bounce of

the sand wedge is maximized, ensuring that the clubhead won't dig too deeply. Be prepared to make a full backswing; the ball won't fly farther than four or five yards. But it will come out with a good deal of backspin—as well as some left-to-right sidespin—and stop within a couple of feet of where it lands. ■

GOLF
MAGAZINE

When there is very little
green between the ball
and the hole, use the flop
sand shot.

*Extremely
open stance*

SAND PLAY

4

High-flying, soft-landing shot

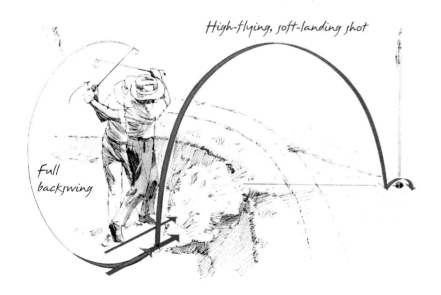

*Full
backswing*

Putting

DEVELOPING TWO DISTINCT STROKES

VISUALIZING THE LINE

CONTROLLING PUTTER SPEED

STAYING RELAXED OVER THE BALL

BETTER USE OF THE LAG PUTT

OVERCOMING THE YIPS

READING THE BREAKS

DEVELOPING TWO DISTINCT STROKES

There are two basic types of putts: Long ones, which you want to get close enough for an easy tap-in; and short ones, 10 feet and less, which you want to hole. It makes sense, then, that there should be two basic types of putting strokes: The long, flowing stroke is well-suited to long putts when distance is important; the short "pop" stroke works best for short putts, when you have to keep the ball on line.

THE LONG STROKE

The long stroke is just that: Long and flowing, with a slow, easy tempo. Take a wide stance and stand a little taller to get a better view of the line. Grip lightly and swing with the arms and shoulders. Keep the wrists quiet, the head and body still. Feel the putterhead swing like a pendulum. Don't worry as much about direction as you do about making solid contact and putting a good roll on the ball.

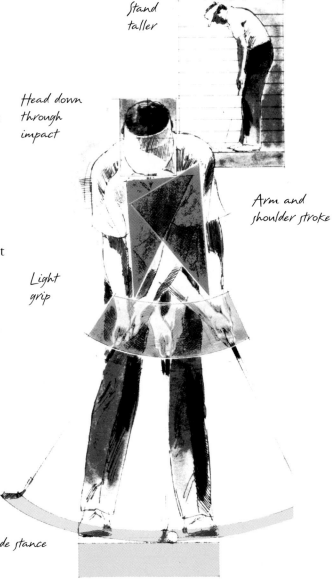

Stand taller

Head down through impact

Arm and shoulder stroke

Light grip

Long and flowing stroke

Wide stance

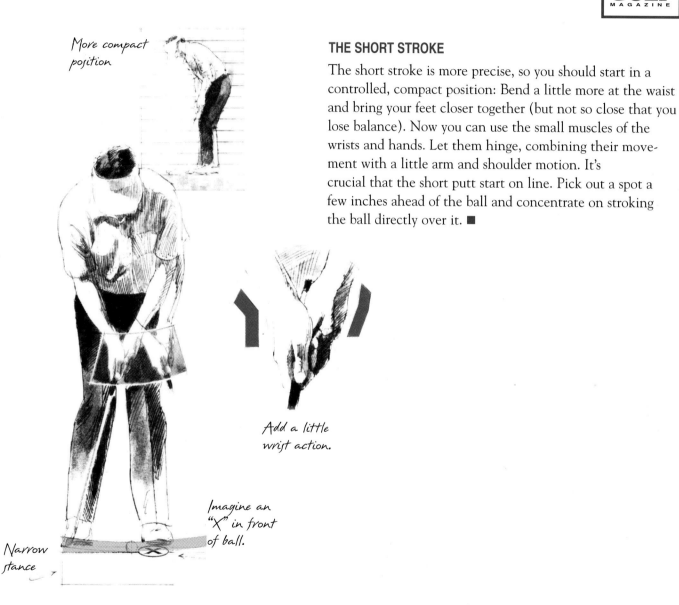

More compact
position

Add a little
wrist action.

Imagine an
"X" in front
of ball.

Narrow
stance

THE SHORT STROKE

The short stroke is more precise, so you should start in a controlled, compact position: Bend a little more at the waist and bring your feet closer together (but not so close that you lose balance). Now you can use the small muscles of the wrists and hands. Let them hinge, combining their movement with a little arm and shoulder motion. It's crucial that the short putt start on line. Pick out a spot a few inches ahead of the ball and concentrate on stroking the ball directly over it. ■

PUTTING

5

VISUALIZING THE LINE

You've probably heard a lot about the importance of visualizing a shot before playing it: Imagining how it will feel coming off the club and how it will look flying to the target. "Seeing" the shot is an important part of the preshot routine of most skilled players. Visualization shouldn't stop when you reach the green. Being able to "see" the line the ball will take is sure to help you. If every putt were straight, picturing the line wouldn't be hard (for that matter, neither would putting), but as you know, it's a rare putt that doesn't have some break to it. If you're having trouble seeing the line, this lesson is for you.

SHARPEN YOUR FOCUS

Practice forming a good mental picture by working with a physical picture first. Get to the practice green while it's still covered with dew. Find a place where the dew is untouched and stroke a 15-footer. Leave the path the first ball cuts untouched and place another ball at its head. Stand behind this ball as if reading a putt and concentrate on the line, then step up to the ball, glance at the line one more time and stroke the ball. Repeat this twice more, then move five feet closer to the cup and go through the same procedure with three more putts on the same line. Move five feet closer and hit three five footers, all the time ingraining the image of the line in your mind.

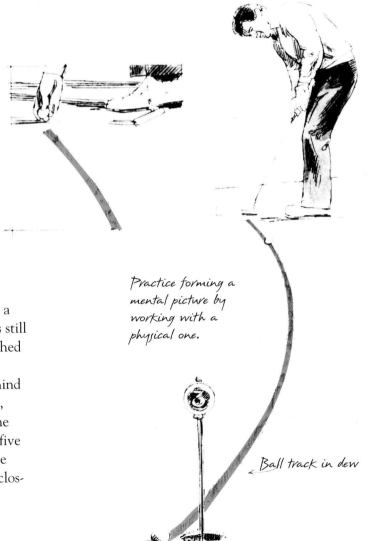

Practice forming a mental picture by working with a physical one.

Ball track in dew

Drop a ball from the bridge of your nose to see if your eyes are over the line.

EYES OVER THE LINE

You'll have a better chance of seeing a line if your eyes are directly over it. To find out if yours are positioned properly, address a putt, then without moving your feet, place two balls next to the original—one directly in front, the other in back. Without your putter, assume your address again and bring a ball up so it touches the bridge of your nose (between your eyes). Let it drop straight down. If it hits any of the three balls, your eyes are over the line. If not, adjust yourself until you can pass this test.

DRILL: Down the Line

If you aren't out early enough to catch the dew, you can still practice seeing the line.

- Stroke a fifteen-foot putt, carefully observing its line.

- Place five balls along the line, three feet apart.

Stroke the one closest to the hole, then quickly go to the next and strike it, keeping the path of the last putt clearly in mind. ∎

CONTROLLING PUTTER SPEED

When your green game goes south, chances are it's not faulty mechanics, but speed control that is off. Break and direction only come into play if the ball is traveling at the right speed. Many, if not most, of your missed putts are hit too far or too short to have any chance to go in. Here are some tips to keep in mind to improve your sense of speed.

HAVE ONE RHYTHM

Your feel for speed can be heightened by establishing a consistent rhythm in your putting stroke, regardless of the length of putt. Find a count to describe your stroke, for example: a-one (backswing) and a-two (downswing). Stay committed to that count on every putt, lengthening the stroke, but not the rhythm, as the putts get longer.

TRY A METRONOME

One way to help establish the right rhythm for your putting stroke is to take a metronome to the practice green. Start with a five-foot putt that you can make fairly easily. Hit 20 or more to get into a groove. Then start experimenting with different rates on the metronome until you find one that matches the rhythm you've established. When you have, keep the metronome ticking as you move the ball

Establish a consistent rhythm regardless of the length of the putt.

Experimenting with different rates on a metronome will help you establish rhythm for various length putts.

To enhance the image of how far the ball must travel, run your eyes from the ball to the hole and back before you make your stroke.

farther and farther from the hole. Practice all kinds of putts—long, short, breakers—matching the rhythm of your stroke to the tick-tock of the metronome.

FOCUS ON DISTANCE DURING PRESHOT ROUTINE

Make speed control the priority during your preshot routine by focusing on distance. Don't get too hung up with the line; read the break, align yourself, and make a practice stroke if you need to. Then address the ball, and run your eyes up the target line to the hole. Pause for a beat, then run your eyes back down from the hole to the ball. Don't wait too long before making your stroke. The idea is to keep the image of how far the ball must travel fresh in your mind as you make your stroke, which will help you get the speed right. ■

PUTTING

5

STAYING RELAXED OVER THE BALL

Most weekend players focus too much on distance, and don't spend enough time on the practice green. As a result, their putting is often erratic, which leads to tension. This causes bad strokes and missed putts.

READ THE LINE

Uncertainty is a major cause of tension. You should know how your putt will break as you set up. If not, your stroke will be tentative and the results inconsistent. Before you putt, check the line from behind the ball. If you don't see it right away, look from behind the hole or from the side (don't take too long). Know exactly where you want the ball to go, over a spot or along an imaginary line, and trust your read.

BEND THE KNEES

Many golfers lock their knees during the stroke. Inconsequential? No. Locking any joint contracts the muscles in that area and creates tension. As a result, your balance suffers. You're much more likely to sway or rock off the ball, resulting in poor contact and errant putts. Keep your knees slightly flexed to steady your body during the stroke.

Keep your knees slightly flexed.

TAP THE PUTTERHEAD

Putting can be such a mechanical motion that many golfers become "locked in," freezing over the ball before stroking it. Making the first move back becomes a real chore, and the result is usually an uneven, herky-jerky stroke that is difficult to control. A great way to avoid tension is by tapping the ground with the putterhead as you stand at address. Once you've aligned yourself and the putterface to the target, lift the putter a half-inch off the ground and let it drop. Repeat a few times, then stroke the ball. This keeps your body in motion, if only slightly, which prevents stiffening up.

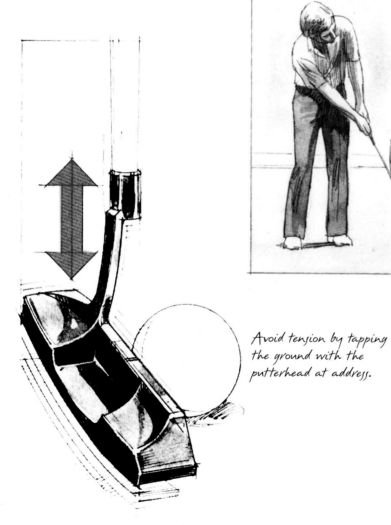

Visualizing someone's smooth stroke will create a positive image for your own.

Avoid tension by tapping the ground with the putterhead at address.

VISUALIZE "MR. SMOOTH"

Whose putting stroke do you envy? The long, silky stroke of Ben Crenshaw? The compact, efficient "pop" of Paul Azinger? Maybe it's another player at your club. Whoever it is, chances are he has a smooth, even tempo that indicates a tension-free motion. That's a good image to have in your head as you stroke your own putt. Visualizing Mr. Smooth's aesthetically pleasing stroke puts you in a positive state of mind over the ball. You'll be more relaxed, and more likely to recreate the smooth stroke in your mind. ■

PUTTING

5

BETTER USE OF THE LAG PUTT

If your problem is pinpoint accuracy, then it's likely you hit a lot of greens just well to one side or the other of your ultimate target, the hole. That means you're probably left with many a lengthy putt, the kind you're glad just to roll up close, tap in, and walk away with par. So if you can't successfully lag long putts close, you're in for a lot of frustration, as well as wasted strokes.

DON'T STRESS OUT

The prospect of three-putting usually causes a player to tense up mentally and physically. The hands, wrists, and forearms get tight as you try to control the putterhead; it's similar to trying to steer the clubhead when faced with a full shot to a tight landing area. Both "steering" and "controlling" lead to poor results. On the green, you produce a poor swing path and a jerky or decelerating stroke. You must learn to relax and let the putterhead go. Take a deep breath, let it out, then release so it swings freely. Concentrate on feeling the weight of the clubhead. Let it coast to a stop on the backswing, then swing it forward at the same speed you swung it back on. Don't control the putter, let it swing.

You'll find that your instincts have a better sense for distance and direction than you do.

MAGNIFYING YOUR MISTAKES

Because you're making a bigger stroke on a long putt, mistakes will be compounded: Mishit a 10-footer and it comes up two feet short; but mishit a 50-footer and it stops 10 feet short. So it's imperative that you keep your body and head still to ensure that the clubface returns to the ball solidly.

On lengthy putts you must learn to relax.

Let the putter coast to a stop on the backswing, then swing it forward at the same speed you swung it back.

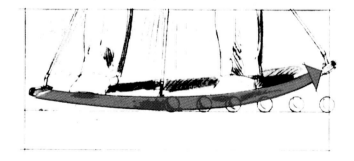

FIND AN INTERMEDIATE TARGET FOR SPEED AND AIM

The hardest thing about rolling the ball close is getting the distance right. Most people gauge a putt's distance by how hard they have to hit it. Instead, pick an intermediate target—a spot on the green on your intended line about 10 feet in front of the ball—and calculate what speed the ball should be rolling when it reaches that spot so it will lose momentum near the cup. Imagine what would be too fast, too slow, and just right. Stroke the ball toward the spot at the speed you've determined.

DRILL: Close Your Eyes

To free your stroke and develop feel for speed on long putts, putt "blind:" Take your address, look at the hole, look at the ball, then close your eyes and make your stroke. Your sense of how fast to swing the putter is much more acute with your eyes closed. ∎

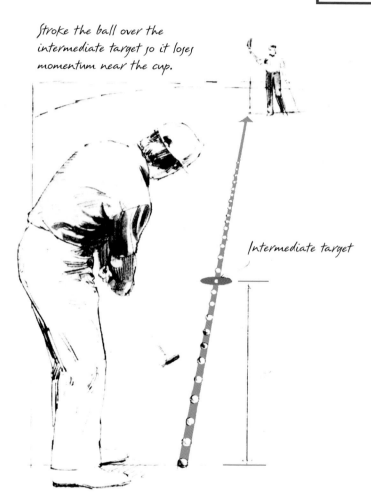

Stroke the ball over the intermediate target so it loses momentum near the cup.

Intermediate target

OVERCOMING THE YIPS

The yips—when it seems next to impossible to make short putts—are treated as a mysterious mental disease in the golf world. But ask most professionals and they'll give you a simple reason for the yips: deceleration. It's very common: Nerves cause you to try to control the clubhead on the throughstroke, rather than letting it swing through impact. As a result, the putter slows down into impact, often closing the clubface and sending the ball left of the target. If you're missing short putts this way, you don't need a psychiatrist. Here are a few drills to help you stop decelerating.

HEAD START

On the practice green, set yourself up for a straight three-foot putt. Once in your address position, replace the ball along the target line about six inches closer to the hole. Now start the backstroke with the putter where it would be for the original putt, then swing it forward and hit the ball. By moving the ball forward, you're forced to keep the clubhead accelerating through what would be the impact zone. Hit a dozen or so putts with the ball forward, then move it back to its original position and feel how your stroke is different.

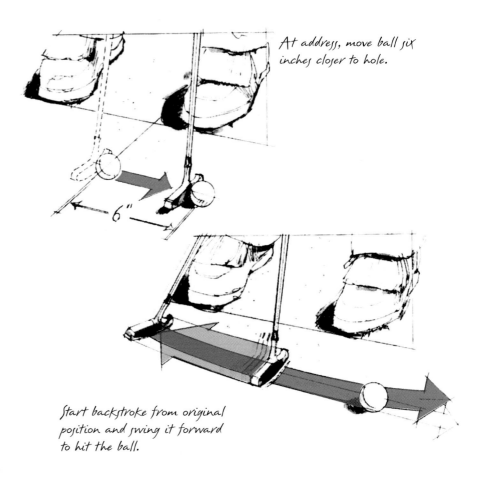

At address, move ball six inches closer to hole.

6"

Start backstroke from original position and swing it forward to hit the ball.

BACKSTOP

Set a ball 10 feet from the hole. Place another ball five inches behind the first one, directly on the target line. Address the first ball and make a backswing, stopping just short of the second ball; swing through and hit the first one. Shortening your backstroke encourages acceleration through impact. The backstroke may be a bit shorter than what you want on the course, but as a drill it will ingrain the proper feeling of clubhead acceleration.

THE PENDULUM

The purest accelerating stroke is the pendulum, where the only force propelling the club forward is the pull of gravity. You can't be quite that pure in your stroke, but it's a good idea to approach that feeling. In your stance, hold the end of the putter grip between your left thumb and forefinger, thumb on top and forefinger underneath. With your right thumb and forefinger, pull back on the bottom of the grip so the putterhead swings back along the target line. To make it swing through, simply let go with the right hand (this is very easy with a long putter). Pay close attention to the rhythm and tempo of the follow-through. After a couple of putts, try to create the same feeling with your regular stroke. ■

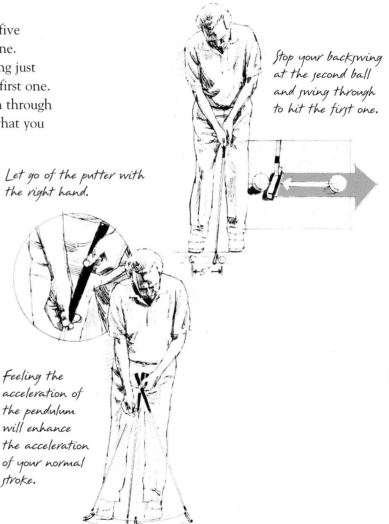

Stop your backswing at the second ball and swing through to hit the first one.

Let go of the putter with the right hand.

Feeling the acceleration of the pendulum will enhance the acceleration of your normal stroke.

PUTTING

5

READING THE BREAKS

If the course you play features sloping greens, you probably face quite a number of sharp-breaking putts each round. To stop three putting big breakers, try these tips.

KNOW THE SPEED FACTORS

The degree of slope isn't the only factor in figuring how much a putt will break. The speed of the putt plays a big part as well. If the green is fast, you don't hit the ball as hard but then, rolling more slowly, it breaks down the slope more than you might expect. On a slow green, you stroke the ball harder so it holds the line over a longer distance before it begins taking the break. In this case, you needn't start the ball quite as much on the high side. The same formula applies to uphill and downhill breakers of the same speed. Downhill, more break; uphill, less break. On bermuda greens, which tend to be grainy, look at the direction of the grain: If it's with the slope, the putt will break more; grain growing against the slope means a little less break.

EVERY PUTT IS "STRAIGHT"

Once you've determined the break, you know the starting line of the putt—the first few feet the ball rolls before being influenced by the slope. Learn to concentrate on the starting line and forget about the hole. Imagine you have a straight putt along the starting line to a hole farther down that line. Resist the tendency to help by pushing or pulling the ball off

Read the break factors carefully,9 then putt to a "hole" that's along your standing line.

the starting line and toward the real hole. If you do steer it, you'll probably miss on the low side. Find the starting line and keep your putter blade moving along that initial path. You'll see more breaking putts going down in two. ■

Power

BUILDING A BIG SWING

HITTING THE LONG BALL

DRILLS FOR POWER AND DISTANCE

CONSISTENT BALL STRIKING

ANOTHER WAY OF GENERATING POWER

FINDING YOUR POWER SOURCE

BUILDING A BIG SWING

A compact, controlled swing lets you keep the ball in play, but it doesn't go miles down the fairway. You can build a bigger swing—one that generates more clubhead speed—if you're willing to trade a little control for more yardage.

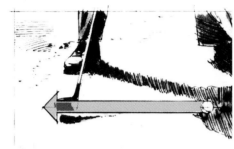

Start the club back on a flat, shallow path, on a straight line away from the ball.

WIDEN YOUR ARC

Don't confuse building a bigger swing with making a longer backswing. The object is to widen the arc on which the clubhead travels so the clubhead moves in a bigger circle. A wide arc begins with the takeaway. Set up with a firm, not stiff, left side and slowly push the clubhead away from the ball on a straight line. (It helps if you think of the clubhead as a heavy chunk of lead.) Keep the clubhead moving on a straight line as long as you can (about a foot-and-a-half is good) by keeping your left arm extended and letting your right arm fold under. As your shoulders turn, the club naturally moves to the inside. Extend your left arm straight back until it's halfway back—at the 9 o'clock position. Guard against reaching too much, which results in swaying off the ball, by keeping your weight on the inside of your right foot.

The larger the arc, the greater the clubhead speed.

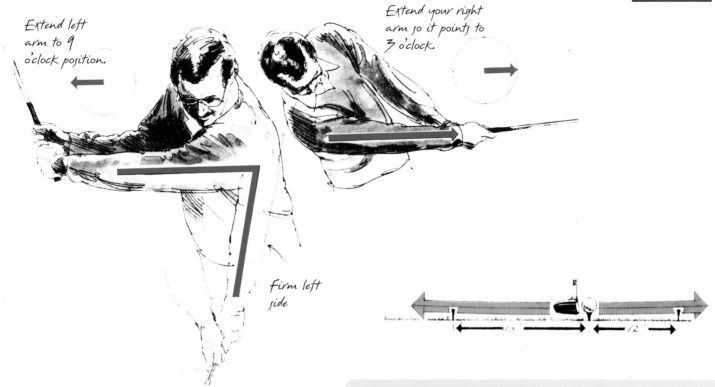

Extend left arm to 9 o'clock position.

Extend your right arm so it points to 3 o'clock.

Firm left side

EXTEND THROUGH IMPACT

A wide backswing arc sets up a wide arc coming down. Maintain your power through the hitting zone by extending the right arm so it points straight at the target—the 3 o'clock position. Pretend you're trying to throw the club-head off the shaft toward your target and you'll keep the clubhead on path longer and create more solid contact.

DRILL: Three Tees to a Wider Arc

Tee the ball normally. Stick a second tee along the target line about 18 inches behind the first; plant a third tee (as shown) about 12 inches in front of the first. On the take-away, knock down the second tee by keeping the club extended, swinging on a shallow path, widening your arc. To further encourage extension through impact, knock the third tee down. ■

HITTING THE LONG BALL

No matter how far you hit it, there are times when you have the impulse to step up and kill the ball—make a gorilla swing. It's a risk, but with these adjustments you should be able to pull it off.

LENGTHEN THE LEFT THUMB

Instead of tucking the left thumb high on the grip, push it down so it looks long, like a hitchiker's. Extending the left thumb as far as it will go down the shaft puts the grip more in the fingertips of the left hand and frees the wrist for a full range of motion. The wrists can then make their maximum contribution to power production.

LEFT FOOT BETWEEN 10 AND 11 O'CLOCK

A counterclockwise rotation of the left hip during the downswing—called clearing—is the essence of the lower body's contribution to power. To make sure your rotating hip is not fighting a restricting left foot, toe your foot out between 10 and 11 o'clock, or about 45 degrees. As you start your downswing, your left hip can turn through unencumbered, allowing the arms and club to whip into the ball.

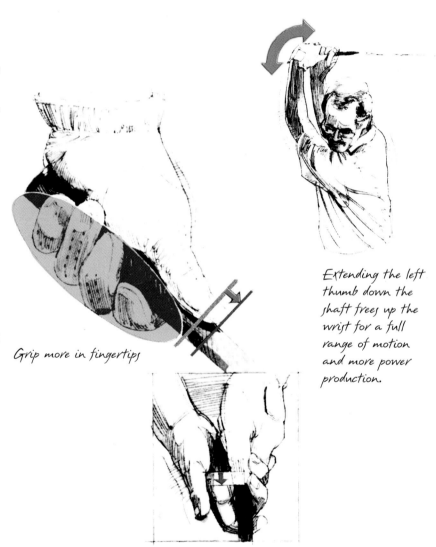

Grip more in fingertips

Extending the left thumb down the shaft frees up the wrist for a full range of motion and more power production.

TEE IT UP AND TEE IT HIGH

Adjust the way you tee the ball for a big drive. First, you want to avoid making a descending blow, because you'll create too much backspin and too little roll. So, instead of playing the ball off your left heel, move it up an inch to your left toe. This ensures that you clip the ball off the tee on a level path or slightly on the upswing for maximum carry and roll. Second, tee the ball a half-inch higher than normal. You may feel that you'll go underneath it, but your swing will adjust to the higher tee by approaching the ball on a flatter plane. You'll find it easier to take the ball from right to left. Chances are you'll also find it more powerful because you'll be swinging around your body. ∎

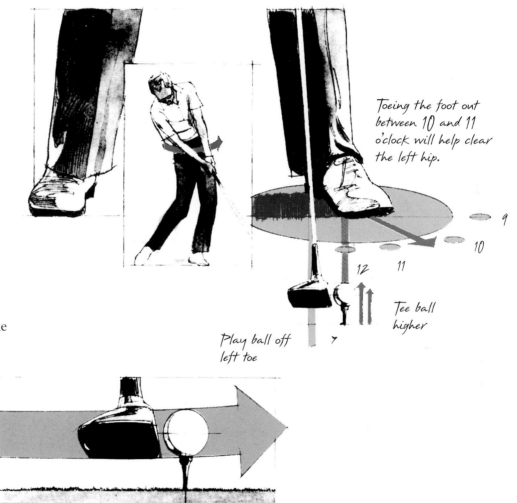

Toeing the foot out between 10 and 11 o'clock will help clear the left hip.

9

10

11

12

Tee ball higher

Play ball off left toe

Ball hit on level path for maximum carry and roll

DRILLS FOR POWER AND DISTANCE

There are a number of technical adjustments you can make to add a few yards here and there to your game. But what if you dream of making a big step in distance, enough to allow you to reach the longer holes in regulation, say, 20 yards with the driver and 15 yards with your approaches. Impossible? No. Significantly lengthening your game requires work to strengthen specific "golf muscles" that will help you become "stronger through the ball." That doesn't mean weightlifting in the gym: With diligent effort and equipment you probably own, two simple drills will add power to your ball-striking.

THE LEAD-HAND DRILL

Have you ever hit a golf ball with only your lead hand? (Left hand for right-handed players, right hand for lefties.) If not, you might be surprised at how tough it is to make clean contact and get the ball airborne. This exercise is designed to build the "pulling" muscles of your left arm and shoulder—the triceps, deltoid and trapezius muscles in particular, which pull the club down through impact. Start the lead-hand

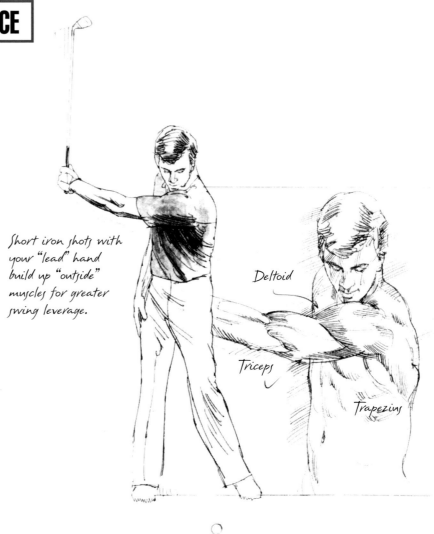

Short iron shots with your "lead" hand build up "outside" muscles for greater swing leverage.

Deltoid

Triceps

Trapezius

drill slowly and progress gradually. Use a pitching wedge and swing easily with your left hand before hitting the ball. The one-handed backswing will go no more than three-quarters of its normal distance. When you're loose and ready to hit the ball, tee it up, even with the wedge. The clubhead speed with the one-handed swing is much slower than normal. You'll feel some shock at impact. Teeing the ball avoids more jarring contact with the ground. Don't try to do too much at one session. Hitting 25 balls with one hand is a good workout for most golfers. Keep hitting the wedge until you can hit it consistently well, then drop down to, say, an 8-iron. Be sure to use a tee. After a few practice sessions you'll see a new verve—and more yards—in your shots.

WEIGHT AND SEE

Swinging a weighted club is a good off-season drill to do in the garage or outside if the weather's not too cold. Use a special heavyweight practice club or a regular club with a weighted cover or a practice "donut" that fits around the neck. Swing the club slowly and easily for 5-10 minutes; 50 swings a day is about right. The extra weight on the end of the club is effective in stretching the back muscles, which leads to a fuller turn. After a month or two of relaxed swinging, most golfers will make a larger arc without loss of control. And a few extra inches of clubhead windup yields

Donut

Slow, steady swinging with a weighted club increases the backswing turn for a distance boost.

more than a few extra yards off the tee. Once again, don't overdo it. Be regular in your sessions, working until you reach the point of slight fatigue rather than pain. ■

CONSISTENT BALL STRIKING

When you're struggling with your distance, solid, consistent ball-striking should be a top priority if you want to keep your game sharp. But how do you practice hitting the ball solidly? Plenty of time grooving your swing on the range helps, of course, but here's a drill for square contact that you can do in any open area. All you need are two tees and a 5-iron. Sole the 5-iron and stick the two tees in the ground, bracketing the clubhead—one about a quarter-inch outside the heel and the other a quarter-inch outside the toe. Take your stance with the clubhead between the two tees, then swing. The idea is to swing through the tees without hitting them, which would indicate a square hit. Doing this drill without a ball eliminates all "hit" impulses and allows you to focus on the swing as one complete, flowing motion. Start with short swings. Using pitch-shot strokes, practice swinging through the tees until you can swing the club back and forth, over and over, without hitting them. Then gradually work your way up to full swings. By the time you can repeat full swings without hitting the tees, you will have had an effective practice session. ■

Swinging through two tees without hitting them indicates a square hit and makes for good practice.

ANOTHER WAY OF GENERATING POWER

A lack of flexibility means a smaller turn, which usually results in a loss of clubhead speed and distance. But be aware that the shoulder turn is not the only link to clubhead speed. Your hands and arms can take over the work, and losing flexibility does not have to cost precious yards. Make whatever turn you can and work on increasing flexibility, paying special attention to using other parts of your body to create clubhead speed. Keep your grip pressure light and your arms soft; you may not be able to get the club parallel to the ground with your turn, but allowing your left elbow to bend slightly and fully cocking your wrists will help give you a wide arc. Stay light on your feet, as well; allowing your weight to shift to the right side is crucial to loading up for a powerful downswing. Starting down, feel your weight shift onto the outside of the left foot as you accelerate the clubhead through the hitting area with your hands and arms. The looser and softer they are, the faster the club will swing and the farther the ball will go. ∎

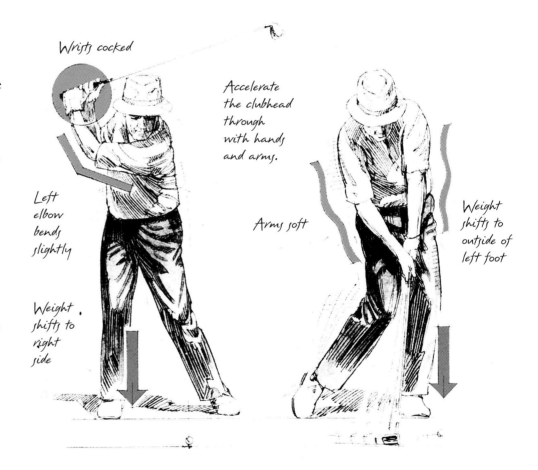

Wrists cocked

Accelerate the clubhead through with hands and arms.

Left elbow bends slightly

Arms soft

Weight shifts to right side

Weight shifts to outside of left foot

FINDING YOUR POWER SOURCE

No doubt you're familiar with the search for more distance. But are you going about it the right way? Each golfer has his or her own physical capabilities: One player might need to widen his swing arc to get more yards, while a player with shorter arms must look elsewhere for power. The search for more yards is much more productive if you know where to look. The first step is to identify your power source.

THE BASIC THREE

The golf swing can be broken down into three primary sources of power: torso rotation, arm swing, and hand action. Depending on your build and flexibility, you should concentrate your efforts in one of these three areas.

SHORT AND STOUT: HAND ACTION

Players with shorter arms and limited flexibility must rely on good hand action through impact to create clubhead speed. Rather than trying to magically create a larger turn or big arc, work on maximizing your strong point. A few nuances in the grip will help. First, a strong left-hand grip, with three knuckles showing at address, gives you more freedom to hinge and unhinge the wrists during the swing. Second, pay close attention to grip pressure: The lighter you hold the club, the more active your hands will be. Third, consider slightly thinner grips, as they put more of the club in your fingers and encourage more hand action.

For the less flexible player, good hand action through impact creates clubhead speed.

Use a strong left-hand grip and light grip pressure

Back straight

Chin up

For long-limbed players, a full extension going back guarantees a wide arc.

Creating space between the hands and body makes room for a powerful arm swing.

LONG AND LEAN: WIDER ARC

Long-limbed players should take advantage of the extra centrifugal force that can be generated by their long arms. It's called making a wide arc, and it starts with the set-up: Be sure your back is straight (tilted forward) and your chin is high rather than tucked into your chest. This enables the arms to swing and the shoulders to turn. The thought on the takeaway is to drag the club straight back along the target line. If you can reach a fully extended position halfway back, with the clubshaft parallel to the target line, you've virtually guaranteed yourself a wide arc. From there, lift your arms to the top of the swing, as the wrists naturally hinge and the shoulders continue to turn. Creating space between your hands and body on the backswing gives you room to swing your arms on the downswing.

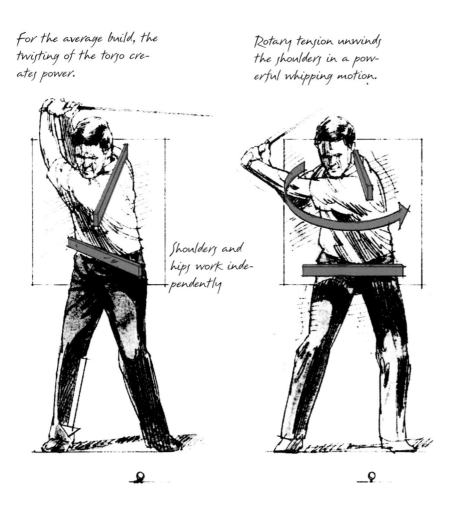

For the average build, the twisting of the torso creates power.

Rotary tension unwinds the shoulders in a powerful whipping motion.

Shoulders and hips work independently

AVERAGE BUILD: TORSO ROTATION

Players with average builds can get extra power from effectively rotating the torso during the swing. It's not just as simple as a big turn, though. A big turn is nice, assuming the weight is firmly planted on the inside of the right foot on the backswing, but it doesn't guarantee power. Power comes from torque, the twisting motion of the torso. To create torque and whip the clubhead through impact, the shoulders and hips must work independently. At the beginning of the downswing, your goal should be to create as much separation between the hips and shoulders as possible: As the left hip rotates through the ball, the shoulders stay wound up as long as possible. The longer the shoulders stay wound, the more separation there is between the hips and shoulders. Finally, there is so much rotary tension that the shoulders are forced to unwind, bringing the arms and club with them in a powerful whipping motion. ■

Shotmaking

FUNDAMENTALS OF SHOTMAKING

It's not enough simply getting the ball airborne. To make strides toward a better game, you must establish some command over your shots, making them fly toward the target in a manner that suits the situation. That's called shotmaking: The better you become, the more you'll find yourself using it—and the more you use it, the better you'll get. The first step to shotmaking is controlling trajectory. Start with a wedge. Sometimes you'll need to hit it low (to make the ball run or fight a headwind) or high (to land it softly or fly over a tree). Here's how to create these shots.

LOW SHOTS: READY, AIM, FIRE!

To shoot a pistol at a target, you don't hold the gun in close to your body; you extend it fully toward the target. This principle also holds true for low golf shots: With your feet pointing slightly left of target to encourage a descending blow, and the ball just behind center in your stance, swing through and extend your arms toward the target. Extending the arms releases the club and prevents the face from opening through impact, which would create a higher flight. As a rule of thumb, for a low shot don't let your arms get above the shoulders on the follow-through.

In pistol shooting you extend the gun fully toward the target.

Open stance, ball behind center

For a low shot extend your arms toward the target.

Lower, hotter flight

To give a bird you are holding a boost into the air, you would throw your hand skyward.

Reach for the sky on your follow-through.

Higher, softer flight

HIGH SHOTS: REACH FOR THE SKY

If you were holding a bird in your hands and wanted it to soar into the air, would you simply let it go? No. You'd throw it up so your hands finished high above your head, reaching for the sky. You'd be giving the bird a boost. Same goes for high shots. Adopt a square stance with the ball slightly ahead of center, and reach for the sky on your follow-through. Striving for a high finish creates a level angle of attack, making the most of the club's loft. ■

Square stance, ball ahead of center

HOW AND WHEN TO WORK THE BALL

You know that working the ball (intentionally hitting shots from right-to-left or left-to-right) is an important tool of good shotmaking. But when should you work the ball? Can't you sometimes hit it straight? Three examples follow that will help you plot your shotmaking strategy.

1) HOLE AT THE BOTTOM OF THE HILL

You're facing a green that slopes from right to left, with the pin tucked behind a trap at the bottom of the hill. Your initial thought may be to follow the natural shape of the hole and draw the ball around the bunker. Think again. Because the green slopes from right-to-left, any similar shot will bounce sharply to the left upon hitting the putting surface and then keep rolling. With little room to miss left of the pin, a draw is not the percentage shot.

The shot to play is a slight fade. Aim at the pin and let the ball move a few yards right. If the shot comes off as planned, your ball lands just right of the pin, and the left-to-right fade spin prevents a sharp kick to the left. If you fade the ball a bit too much, there's little chance of missing the green right, because the slope to the left won't allow for much roll. Playing the fade leaves you more margin for error and a better chance of hitting the green. So consider the contours of the green as well as pin position when picking a shot shape.

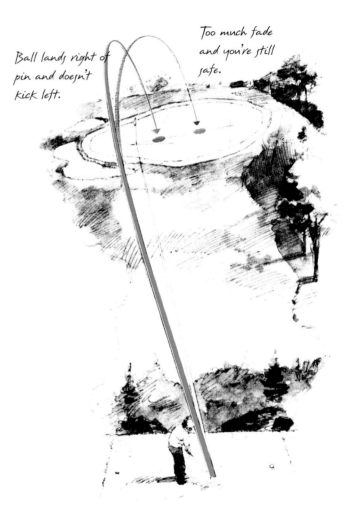

Ball lands right of pin and doesn't kick left.

Too much fade and you're still safe.

Aim at the pin and let the ball fade a few yards to the right.

2) PIN BACK LEFT

This time you should play the draw, assuming there's no severe slope to direct the ball into the bunker on the left. The trick is picking your target. On the one hand, you could aim three yards right of the pin and try to draw it toward the hole, but if you're short, you're in the bunker. On the other hand, if you aim 10 yards right and try to draw it, a short shot leaves you on the front of the green facing a relatively routine two-putt. Plus, you have seven extra yards to play with. When working the ball, always aim at a point that provides the most options for hitting the green.

3) DON'T BE A SUCKER

Picture the green with the pin tucked behind the right bunker. Do you fade the ball around the bunker to the pin? Sucker! See that stream running to the right of the green? It will catch any ball that lands right of the green, which means penalty strokes and double bogeys. A pin set near the right edge of the green tempts the better golfer to flirt with both the bunker and the water. That's a "sucker" pin placement, requiring an almost perfect shot with no margin for error. This is a situation where you don't want to get fancy. Besides the trouble right, there's a bunker on the left. The smart shot is simply to the middle of the green, between the bunkers. You must be patient when the pin position makes double bogey a possibility; play for par and let the birdies come later. ■

A short shot leaves you on the front of the green.

Aim ten yards to the right of the pin and draw the shot.

The smart shot is to the middle of the green.

LOFTING LONG IRONS

Hitting a long iron on a low trajectory is a good strategy in a strong headwind. Most of the time, though, you'll want to hit a more controlled high shot that lands softly and holds the green. Here's how to get your irons up.

PROPER BALL POSITION

Playing the ball forward in the stance—one inch behind the left heel—is the most important set-up key, for it allows you to sweep the ball, whereas playing the ball back causes you to hit with a descending blow. You also may find it helpful, at address, to tilt your weight slightly back toward your heels, which will help make a shallow, sweeping downswing.

WIDE, WIDE ARC

The wider the swing arc, the higher the shot. To create the widest possible arc, set up with a straight left arm and keep the clubhead low to the ground in the take-away. Feel as if you are stretching the left hand away from your left shoulder while turning around the fixed axis of your spine.

Learn to hit long irons with a high, soft trajectory.

The ball must be forward in the stance.

Stretch the left hand away from the left shoulder.

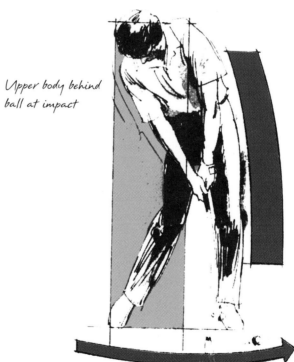

Upper body behind ball at impact

Strong left side

Sweep club through

STAY BEHIND THE BALL

After reaching a parallel position at the top, shift your weight to your left side to start the downswing. Then, as you pull the club through with your hands, keep your upper body behind the ball until impact. Make no effort to help the ball into the air; sweep the club through and finish high. ■

A NEW APPROACH TO DRAWS AND FADES

Most players don't mind when their shots fly straight. However, there will be times when you will want to curve the ball in order to hit a particular side of the fairway or green. Bending the ball requires changes in your set-up and/or swing. The most common method of hitting draws and fades is to align your body to the left or right of the target while keeping the clubface square. But here's another way: Change ball position.

RIGHT-TO-LEFT

To hit a draw, simply move the ball back in your stance a couple of inches. Moving the ball back closes the shoulders relative to the target line. Also, the clubhead will be approaching from the inside as it meets the ball. Provided the clubface is square, the shot will start to the right of the target and draw.

LEFT-TO-RIGHT

To hit a fade, move the ball slightly forward in your stance. This opens the shoulders so the club approaches the ball from out-to-in, producing slice-spin on the ball. Moving the ball forward positions it past the lowest part of the swing. A steep swing will cause the club to hit behind the ball, while a flat one will produce thin shots because the club will be coming up at impact. Keep this in mind, and try to sweep the ball off the turf. As with any new shot, practice on the range before taking it to the course. ■

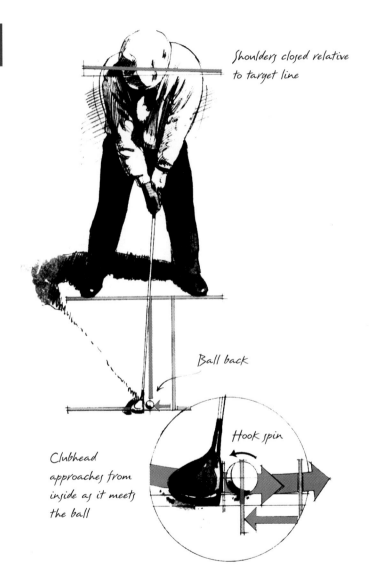

Shoulders closed relative to target line

Ball back

Hook spin

Clubhead approaches from inside as it meets the ball

Shoulders open relative
to target line

Ball forward

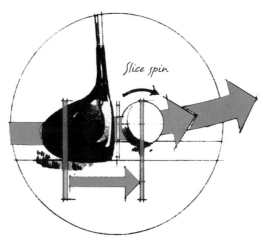

Slice spin

Clubhead approaches from outside
as it meets the ball

INCORPORATING THE PUNCH SHOT

Good golf comes from shotmaking—finding ways to make the ball do what you want. A good start is learning how to hit the punch shot. The punch, or knockdown, as it is sometimes called, is a shot hit with a shorter swing that flies on a lower, more boring trajectory. It's one of the most versatile shots to have in your bag: Use it to fight a headwind when you're in between clubs or from a tricky lie in the rough when control is needed. Here's the basic technique.

MID-IRONS AND UP

The punch shot requires a descending blow, so long irons (which approach the ball on a relatively shallow angle) are out. As a general rule, use any club between a 5-iron and a sand wedge.

EVERYTHING GETS JUST A LITTLE TIGHTER

For a punch 6-iron, narrow your stance so your feet are a hair less than shoulder-width and aligned slightly left of the target. Play the ball between the heels, with your weight favoring the left side. Grip down on the club an inch or two and you're ready to go. Rather than make a full swing, concentrate your weight on your left side and make a three-quarter-length backswing. Pull your hands down into the back of the ball with the feeling that your hands are leading the clubhead into impact. Don't be in a hurry to rotate the

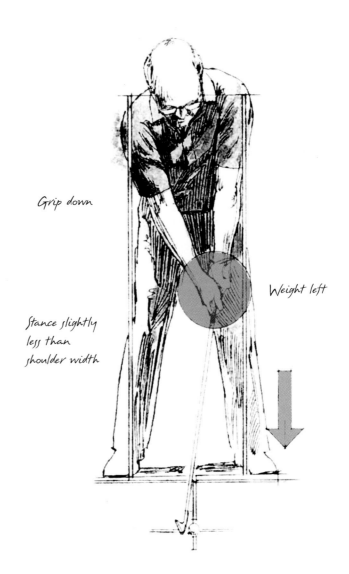

Grip down

Weight left

Stance slightly
less than
shoulder width

arms on the downswing; this may close the clubface and cause a quick snap-hook. Instead, think about keeping the back of the left hand facing the target until after impact, which will keep the clubface square to the target. You should take a divot, and the follow-through should be short. ∎

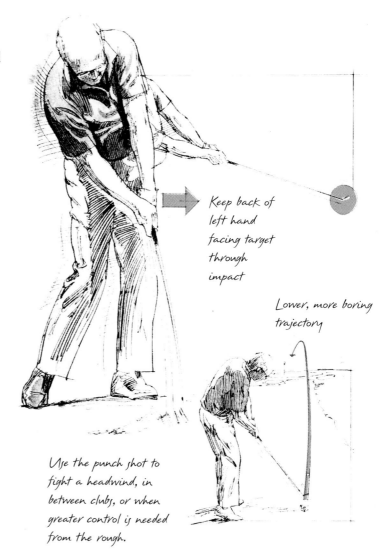

Keep back of left hand facing target through impact

Lower, more boring trajectory

Use the punch shot to fight a headwind, in between clubs, or when greater control is needed from the rough.

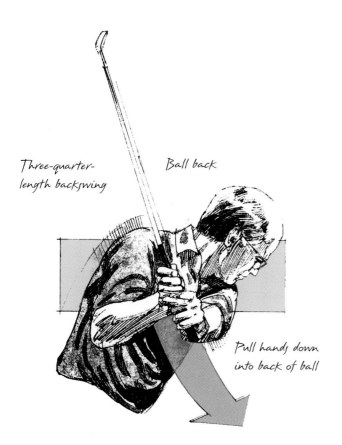

Three-quarter-length backswing

Ball back

Pull hands down into back of ball

DRILLS FOR THE PRACTICE TEE

When you practice, do you hit ball after ball, trying to develop a consistent, repeatable swing? It's a popular training method, but it can easily lead to an overemphasis on mechanics—something that a player with natural ability shouldn't take to the course. Additionally, if you hit 100 balls from one spot, you groove your swing to play from one situation, while on the course, every shot is different. Whether you're working out on the driving range or putting green, your practice sessions will be much more effective if you add variety-practice hitting shots, rather than "the swing," or "the stroke." Try the following practice routine to improve more of your game.

ON THE TEE: WORK THE BALL

Don't ignore mechanics completely; just restrict that focus to your warm-up, when you're trying to find a swing that will provide solid contact. Once you're loose and hitting the ball relatively square, stop thinking about the swing and start working the ball. Aim right, close the clubface slightly, and hit three draws to the 150-yard flag with your 6-iron. Open your stance, take a slightly weaker grip, and fade three drives toward the big tree at the end of the range. Move the ball up in your stance and hit a handful of high 3-irons at the 200-yard flag. Play the ball back and hit a few knockdown 8-irons at the 100-yard flag. Take it a step further. Hit a few shots out of divot holes.

Move the ball up in your stance and hit a few high 3-irons at the 200 yard flag.

Your practice sessions will be more effective if you add variety and practice hitting shots rather than "the swing."

Hit a few knockdown 8-irons at the 100 yard flag.

Find uneven lies and hit from there. Instead of thinking mechanics, you'll be concentrating on using the swing to play your way through different situations. It's much more practical.

Try some shots from divot holes.

Hit the lob shot from a sidehill lie.

Take several clubs and chip from a variety of situations.

Work with a dozen or so balls at a time, trying to one-putt each of them.

AROUND THE GREEN: UP AND DOWNS

Good shotmaking around the green requires creativity, so be creative when you practice too. Don't just drop a bucket of balls at a spot and chip them all to one hole. Mix it up. Take several clubs and use each from a variety of situations. Challenge yourself. If you normally chip with an 8-iron, hit a few standard chips, then try running a few through the rough to the green. Hit some standard pitch shots, then find some hardpan and hit a few from there. Hit the lob shot from a sidehill lie. Keep in mind that on the course, you want to get the ball up and down; have your putter handy. Work with a dozen or so balls at a time, trying to one-putt each of them. Keep working until you get 75 percent of your short shots up and down. ■

The Mental Game

KEEPING A STREAK ALIVE

BUILDING CONFIDENCE THROUGH COMPETITION

MAINTAINING SWING CONSISTENCY

BREAKING THE 80 BARRIER

ESTABLISHING A STEADY RHYTHM

KEEPING A STREAK ALIVE

Making five pars in a row isn't too much to ask of a good golfer. Too often, however, you play five or six holes at even par, realize you're on a hot streak, then come crashing to earth with a double bogey. You must be able to handle a hot streak to become a consistently excellent golfer. Here are some tips to keep a good streak going.

DON'T THINK IN BUNCHES

One common streak-killer is "streak awareness." You're playing well, in a good rhythm, and then you realize you've made four straight pars. Suddenly the question "How many consecutive pars can I make?" becomes more important than "What do I do to execute the next shot?" It takes concentration to remain focused on the shot at hand during a hot streak. Go a little overboard setting up each shot when you're playing well. Picture exactly the kind of shot you want to hit: how it will feel coming off the clubface, what the ball flight will look like, where and how it will bounce when

The feel

The flight

The bounce

Picture exactly the kind of shot you want to hit.

For added excitement, pretend you're playing a "special" hole.

it hits the ground. If you have to, picture yourself in a different surrounding: Pretend you're on the 18th hole at Pebble Beach or the 12th hole at Augusta. That way, every shot will get your full attention.

FOLLOW UP STRONG

Par. Par. Par. Par. Birdie. What's next? If it's double bogey more often than par, your problem isn't talent—it's mental toughness. Don't let the high of making birdie overcome you. Spend the walk from green to tee savoring it, then forget about it! Remain committed to the rhythm and pace that carried you through those good holes. Don't let a birdie change your game plan, either. There's no need to get conservative. Chances are you had to be aggressive to get into the hot streak, so stick with it. It may bring you another birdie. ■

Spend the walk from green to tee savoring your birdie; then forget about it.

BUILDING CONFIDENCE THROUGH COMPETITION

You've worked hard to build a solid game. But now it seems no amount of practice will make you better.

HEADCASE

Usually, the culprit is your mind. Ask yourself the following questions: Have I ever had a career round going only to limp home with bogeys and double bogeys? Do I have trouble putting together two solid nines? Do I play noticeably worse during tournaments? If so, you need to toughen up the mental side of your game by searching out competitive, pressure-filled situations. They are not easy to handle, so you will need to learn to play well under these conditions.

PRACTICE UNDER FIRE

You can't reproduce the pressure of a competitive round, but you can simulate it by having something on the line when practicing. A putting contest, closest-to-the-pin competition, or match with a friend with something at

A match with a friend with something at stake...

Hit 10 consecutive drives inside an imaginary fairway.

A putting contest...

stake will make you concentrate and want to win. You also can practice alone: Stroke 25 consecutive three-foot putts, starting over of you miss one, or hit 10 consecutive drives inside an imaginary fairway. The key to this type of practice is to make your mistakes have consequences. At first, you might find the pressure difficult to handle, but it will become easier as you get used to it. Another note: Constantly challenge yourself. If making three-footers becomes too easy, try four-footers.

IN THE SPOTLIGHT

There's nothing like a tournament to sharpen your mental game. You'll find all kinds of local and national events. Enter as many as possible, but be realistic—don't expect to play as well as usual in your first few outings. There will be many good players at these tournaments, and when you're paired with them, use the opportunity to learn. Don't be intimidated; realize that their games are not much different from yours, and that you are capable of hitting any shot they can. The difference is that they make fewer mistakes and are tougher mentally. However, as you keep playing in tournaments, you will notice your scores going down, both in competition and in casual rounds, as your ability to concentrate and focus improves. ■

Playing in as many tournaments as possible will help sharpen your mental side.

MAINTAINING SWING CONSISTENCY

An old saying is "no one ever owns the secret to golf, they only borrow it for a little while." One day you'll hit the ball beautifully, the next time out you can't hit the broad side of a cart barn. It's not your fault, it's simply the nature of the game. If you want to shoot low scores all the time, you've got to make your swing work reasonably well whenever you play. With your solid grounding in the fundamentals, the key to making your swing work any time, anywhere is having an arsenal of mental swing thoughts to turn to on any given day, for any given shot. A good swing thought adds confidence, and once you've got a good hold of the basics of the game, confidence is the deciding factor between a good round and a mediocre one. Start by writing down a list of swing keys that have worked in the past. Try to remember everything, even if they've worked only once. Johnny Miller calls these "wood" keys, for "works only one day" because they could prove effective again.

"One-piece takeaway"

"Point clubhead to sky"

Be on the lookout for new keys to add to your list when reading about golf, watching on television, or practicing. Don't think this means you'll need a different key every time you play. But most players have favorites that work for them a good part of the time. Be prepared to switch day-to-day, or even mid-round if your game starts to go awry. Be sure to hit balls before playing.

Not only does it warm up your muscles, but it also gives you a chance to feel out your swing and judge your shots for that day. If the ball isn't flying right, use the practice time to come up with the key that will adjust your swing. ■

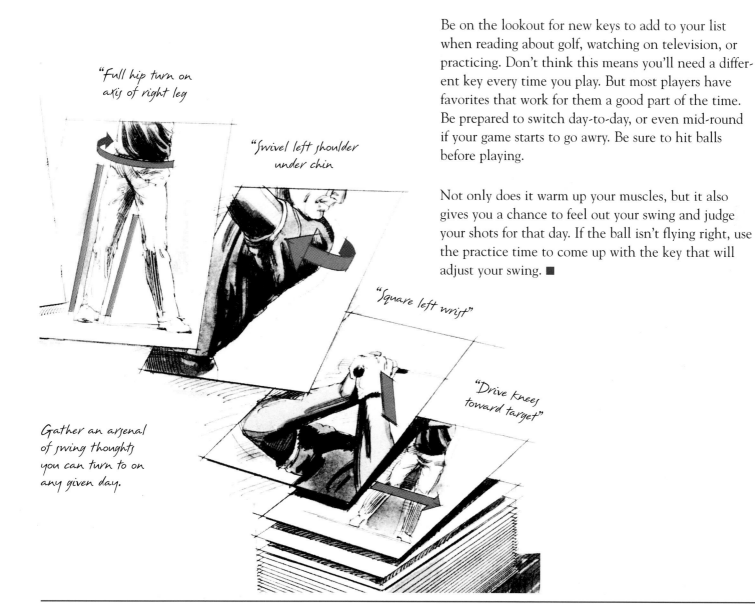

"Full hip turn on axis of right leg

"Swivel left shoulder under chin

"Square left wrist"

"Drive knees toward target"

Gather an arsenal of swing thoughts you can turn to on any given day.

BREAKING THE 80 BARRIER

What does it take to shoot in the 70s? If you can shoot 82, you can just as easily shoot 76. You have the game for it. But do you have the mind? If you're used to shooting 82, 76 is a tall order. To break out of your comfort zone, change your view of the round.

SCORE IN TRIADS

Trying to shoot a target score or sustaining excellent play over 18 holes can put a lot of pressure on you. Instead, break up your round into six groups of three holes. To break 80, set a goal of averaging 13 strokes for each set of three holes. (Six groups times 13 strokes equals 78 strokes). Breaking up the round helps you to stay in the present and not look ahead to difficult holes or ones you might birdie. It also eases the feeling that you must par every hole to break 80. If one group consists of two par fours and a five, try to par them all; if the next triad is three, four, five, you can have a bogey; in a triad of two par threes and a five, you can have two bogeys, and so on, whatever it takes to make 13 strokes. If you score under 13, great; over 13 and you must find a triad (preferably with more than one par three) where you can score under 13. Remember, the goal is to average 13 for each triad. That allows you, on average, a bogey every three holes.

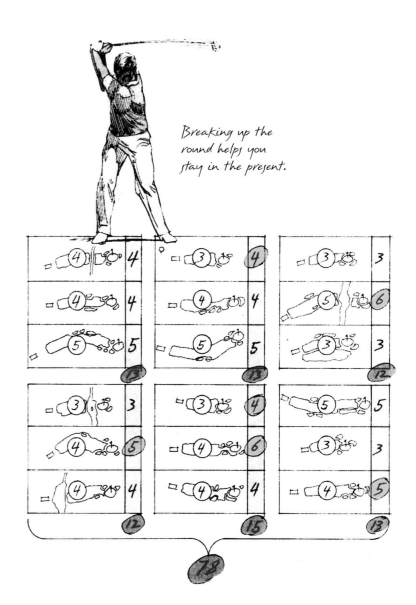

Breaking up the round helps you stay in the present.

BREAK UP YOUR SWING THOUGHTS

The legendary Bobby Jones used to say he never worried about playing his best over the first few holes because he was getting a feel for the course and didn't want his expectations too high before he knew what he could do that day. For you, that means don't saddle yourself with an intricate swing thought on the first tee and attempt to sustain it throughout the round. Use the first six holes to "find your swing." Don't do anything fancy, just advance the ball. Keep it in the fairway, regardless of how your swing feels, and you'll be surprised how easy it is to make pars. After the first six holes, your body will be ready to focus on a swing thought. Pick one that feels right and focuses on the downswing. Backswing keys are position-oriented and often put mechanical thoughts into your head. Downswing thoughts are motion-oriented and focus on the target, which is what you want. Over the last six holes, your objective is sustaining the rhythm developed over the rest of the round. Let your swing key become almost unconscious. Focus on keeping grip pressure light and on a smooth tempo. Staying in control down the home stretch will ensure breaking your comfort zone. ■

Find your swing, advance the ball, and keep it in the fairway.

Focus on a downswing key thought, and the target.

Focus on light grip pressure and tempo.

ESTABLISHING A STEADY RHYTHM

When you play well, you play steady, without a lot of highs and lows—just consistently good results. It can be almost boring, as shot after shot flies predictably at the target. What's enjoyable (besides the numbers on your scorecard) is the feeling of falling into a steady, comfortable rhythm, as if a hum guides your every move. Some people refer to this state as being "in the zone," or "in a groove." Don't make the mistake of thinking a steady rhythm happens when the golf gods bestow it upon you. You can, and must, make it happen for yourself.

HONE IN ON YOUR ZONE

Your first step is discovering your most comfortable rhythm. Often it has something to do with your swing thought. On the one hand, if you're trying to keep your swing slow and smooth, you might find that a leisurely pace suits you best. On the other hand, if you're the kind of player who gets pumped up by playing well, a faster pace would be better.

BE CONSISTENT

Once you've committed to a rhythm, let it permeate everything you do, not only your swing, but the way you walk, tee up your ball,

even speak. Establish the rhythm in all your actions, and it will carry over to your golf swing. You're not going to a hit a perfect shot every time. But, if you are looking to slow down your swing, there's a better chance of success if everything you do is slow and steady, even the way you get dressed for a round or drive to the golf course. If you prefer a quicker rhythm, don't drive fast, but do things to keep a high energy level. Listen to upbeat music on the car radio or tape deck. Arrange your schedule to avoid spending a lot of time waiting around before you play. Maintain a steady rhythm and you're more likely to fall into a successful groove. ■

Once you've committed to a certain rhythm, let it permeate everything you do.

Faults

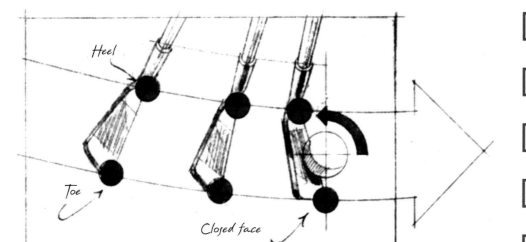

Heel

Toe

Closed face

TURNING SLICES INTO FADES

The fade is a great shot to have, particularly if distance is not your problem. But a gentle fade can become a slice with very little notice. Then once you have it, a slice seems to feed on itself and your adjustments seem to make it even more severe. Here are some checkpoints to help you reclaim that gentle fade.

CHECK YOUR GRIP

Strong players often fall into the habit of turning their hands too far to the left on the club, possibly to prevent hooking. This weak grip makes it difficult to get the clubface back to square at impact, and the ball slides off the open clubface to the right. So place your hands on the club in a neutral position, with the back of the left hand and palm of the right facing the target. The Vs formed by the thumbs and forefingers should point to the inside of your right shoulder.

LINE UP A LITTLE LEFT

Many golfers try to curve the ball by setting up with their bodies pointing drastically left or right of the target. If you're conscious of slicing, the tendency is to aim even further left to allow for it. But fight the urge to aim too far left. Set the leading edge of your clubface square to your target. Carefully align your feet, knees, hips and shoulders just a touch left of your target line. Have a friend stand behind you to confirm

Super-weak grip leads to open clubface

Neutral grip promotes square return of clubface through ball

your alignment. It's too easy to think you're aligning properly when you're really not, particularly when fighting a slice.

DON'T CUT IT

Once you're aligned, you simply swing the club on a normal plane relative to your body line. Don't try picking the club up and to the outside on the backswing or manipulating the clubhead from outside-in on the downswing. If you swing along the plane your body has established, the clubhead will contact the ball while moving just slightly from outside to inside the target line. When you return the clubface squarely to the ball, the shot will start slightly left of the target and drift gently right as it descends. Keep close tabs on your grip and alignment angles and you'll be able to reproduce the controlled fade on shot after shot—and stay consistently in play. ■

Swing normally and let your set-up angles do the work for you.

Set clubface square to target line and make sure your body points just slightly left.

CORRECTING A NAGGING HOOK

A hook can be damaging because the ball runs a long way after landing, putting you deeper into trouble and leaving you in a tough scrambling position either off the fairway or around the green. Correcting a hook isn't always easy. Since your swing is basically sound, the fault likely is subtle and difficult to detect. Nevertheless, here are a few causes and cures to help you straighten out a hook.

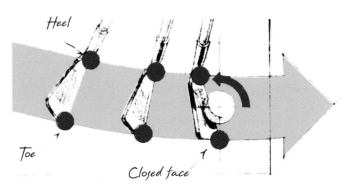

Heel

Toe

Closed face

CLOSED STANCE

The first place to look is at your alignment. Lay one club across your toes, another along the target line and compare the two. If you see that your stance is closed (aiming to the right of the target), square yourself up. A closed stance causes you to swing back on a flat plane and roll your forearms—and the clubface—over too quickly in the hitting area.

INSIDE TAKEAWAY

The clubhead should move slightly to the inside in the takeaway, not deliberately but as a result of your shoulder turn. If you deliberately try to take the club "inside," you're likely to snatch it too far inside the line, causing an inside-out swing, which promotes a hook. To convince yourself that the shoulders can bring the club inside properly, try this experiment: Take your address position a few

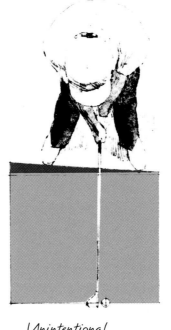

Unintentional closed stance

Clubhead moving abruptly inside

feet from a wall and rest the toe of an iron against the molding. Keep your hands quiet as you turn your shoulders. You'll see that the club moves naturally to the inside, away from the wall.

TOO MUCH RIGHT HAND

When you hear a player grumble, "I used too much right hand" after hitting a hook, he means his right hand overpowered the left on the downswing, causing the clubface to close at impact. Prevent this fault by gripping more firmly with the last two fingers of the left hand, which will keep the left wrist firm through impact. Also, weaken the right hand slightly by turning it a little to the left. This adjustment will allow you to continue hitting hard with the right side without overpowering the left.

STANDING TOO FAR FROM THE BALL

Extending your arms at address may promote a feeling of power, but it also sets up a very flat swing and a hook. You can tell you're standing too far from the ball when you feel your weight creeping toward your toes and tension in your arms. Adjust your set-up by resting the clubhead comfortably behind the ball, setting your weight on the balls of your feet and letting your arms hang freely. Your left arm should be extended but not tense; your right arm should be bent at the elbow and very limp. ■

To combat "too much right hand," take firmer grip with left hand and weaker grip with right.

Standing too far from ball results in flatter swing, causing . . .

forearms to roll too quickly, closing the clubface.

Weight toward toes

F A U L T S

9

AVOIDING THE REVERSE WEIGHT SHIFT

What does your finish position look like? Are you standing tall, facing the target with your weight on your left foot and only your right toe touching the ground? If you're like many players, this does not describe you. Do you instead fall back and finish with your weight on your right foot? This means you've made the dreaded reverse-weight shift. A reverse-weight shift occurs when too much of your weight remains on your left side on the backswing. It is then transferred to the right foot during the downswing, taking power and accuracy out of your motion. In a good backswing, most of your weight goes to the inside of the right foot at the top. The more weight you can shift to your right side, the more potential energy is built up, which then can be transferred to the left side of the downswing.

This weight shift, which is vital to hitting long, straight shots, can only be achieved by getting your weight to the right at the top. Try this swing key when hitting balls to help get your weight back: Turn your left shoulder until it points behind the ball at the top. This means you've made a full turn and a good weight shift.

Weight remains on left side on backswing.

Weight transferred to right foot on downswing.

GOLF
MAGAZINE

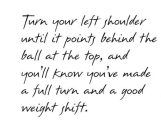

DRILL: Hit Balls on Upslope

To ingrain the feel of making a correct weight shift, hit balls off an upslope, being sure to swing smoothly. The upslope forces the transfer of most of the weight to the right foot at the top. You will have difficulty getting your weight to your left side against the slope, so don't worry much about not being able to do it. Remember the sensation of having your weight on your right side and try to duplicate it when hitting off flat lies. It will make it easier to finish like a pro. ∎

FAULTS

9

Turn your left shoulder until it points behind the ball at the top, and you'll know you've made a full turn and a good weight shift.

FINDING YOUR TEMPO

Tempo is the speed of the swing, the time it takes from the first move in the takeaway to the full finish position. Some players have fast tempos, swinging back and through quickly like Arnold Palmer or Greg Norman. Others make a smooth, deliberate motion, like that of Payne Stewart or Fred Couples. No matter what speed your tempo is—fast or slow—problems will arise the minute you try to swing faster than your natural rhythm allows.

FIND YOUR TEMPO

Before you can determine if you're swinging too fast, you must know your normal tempo when you are swinging "within yourself." To feel your best swing speed, make a practice swing, pretending you are hitting a shot. That swing should feel effortless, balanced and controlled, which is how you want to feel on every shot. Unfortunately, the presence of the ball brings out the speed demons in all of us. Becoming less conscious of the ball will help you learn to hit with your practice swing. Here are two ways to break the ball-bound habit:

1) Hit plastic practice balls. Because they are nearly weightless, there is no discernible feeling at impact, so you stop trying to hit the ball and start swinging the club.

2) Try the hip-high swing. Holding a 5-iron, swing your hands back to hip-height, stop, then swing through to a high finish. Be sure to drive with your legs, not just

Hitting wiffle balls will help you to "swing" the club rather than hit the ball.

Tempo is the time it takes from the first move in the takeaway to the full finish position.

GOLF
MAGAZINE

your hands and arms. You'll find that to get any distance, you have to swing through the ball, not at it. After practicing several shots this way, return to making a full swing. You'll have the right feel in the hitting zone.

FAST FAULTS

A few common mistakes also promote a too-fast swing. A quick takeaway usually results in a quick swing. Be sure your whole body is working in the takeaway, not just the hands and arms. If your takeaway is too quick, start the clubhead's movement by rotating your shoulders and shifting your weight; let the area from the elbows to the fingertips respond to the motion rather than initiate it. The change of direction from the end of the backswing to the start of the downswing is another speed check. Think of the downswing as having a tempo separate from that of the backswing. Set the club in position at the top, pause for a split second, then kick off the downswing by moving the lower body toward your target. Don't think about hitting the ball; think about swinging through impact and finishing high. ∎

Pause for a split-second. . .

Kick off downswing by moving lower body toward target.

Hip-high backswing

Drive through with legs

Hip-high swing also helps you to swing through the ball.

F A U L T S

9

STAYING DOWN THROUGH THE BALL

"Stay down" you mutter after a topped shot. So you stand over the next shot, think "stay down, stay down," and top another one. "Why can't I stay down?" you wonder in frustration. You might be surprised to know that all your efforts to stay down are what's bringing you up and causing topped shots. It starts with your head. Say "Keep your head down," and your chin drops to your chest. But with that, your shoulders droop forward and there's no room to coil your body during the backswing. As a result, you tilt—left shoulder drops toward the ball, right shoulder rises as your arms lift the club to the top. You're stuck. If you swing through in the proper fashion, unwinding the shoulders and hips and letting the arms follow, the club comes over the top on an extremely steep path, probably sticking in the turf behind the ball. To avoid such a fate, your body unconsciously raises up—back straightens, head lifts, you fall away from the ball, and the shot is topped. No surprise considering the unnecessary movement in the swing. To make solid contact consistently, your swing must be balanced and feature no wasted motion: No tilting, lifting, or falling back. Such a swing starts with your set-up.

Head on chest . . . shoulders droop forward

Tilting instead of coiling

To avoid hitting behind ball, body raises up, back straightens, and head lifts.

Club comes over the top on an extremely steep path.

Topped shot

GOLF
MAGAZINE

BE A PUPPET

To ingrain a proper set-up, believe you have no other alternative. Imagine you are a marionette. The puppet master has strings attached to your back, shoulders, and chin. As you address the ball, the puppet master tugs all the strings, making sure that your chin is high, your spine is straight, and your shoulders don't droop. You can't hunch over even if you want to. With your chin high, you are free to rotate your torso around your spine; your arms follow along. On the downswing, no compensation is necessary, and your chances for solid contact are much better. ■

Imagine a puppet master making sure your chin is high and your back is straight.

With your chin high, torso rotates about spine easily.

F A U L T S

9

FIXING COMMON FAULTS

Nobody has a perfect swing; in fact, a lot of good players have "flawed" swings. Some mistakes are excusable. However, no matter what level of player you are, there are mistakes you can't afford to make. Here are a few to watch out for.

WEAK GRIP

Traditional instruction says you should be able to see at least two knuckles on the left hand as you look down at your grip, but don't be fooled. The weaker the grip, the more restricted hand action will be, and only two knuckles showing is somewhat restrictive. Unless you are unusually strong and flexible, you need lively hands to keep your clubhead speed up. When you look down at your left hand, you should see at least 2 1/2 knuckles, and three is by no means too many.

HEAD DROP

Maximizing your upper body turn is tough enough; don't let poor posture make it even tougher. A common mistake is to drop the head at address so the chin nearly touches the neck. This limits the

For less restricted hand action, take a stronger grip.

Chin up, spine straight

Head down and poor posture

Good shoulder turn

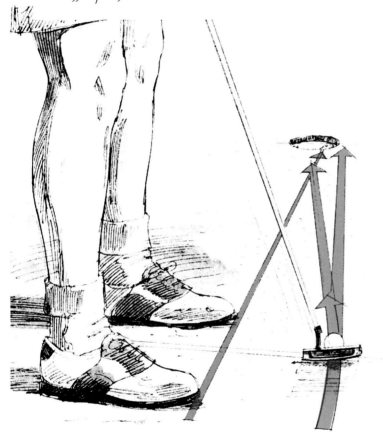

Faulty alignment will lead to clubface manipulation and missed putts.

shoulder turn on the backswing. Pay close attention to your address position: Keep your spine straight and chin up, so there's room for your shoulders to turn on the backswing.

FAULTY PUTTER ALIGNMENT

For many players, putting is the key to better scores. Faulty alignment will kill you on scoring putts of three to 10 feet. The common mistake is to line up to the right of the hole, then close the clubface during the forward stroke to redirect the ball back toward the hole. When you feel the pressure of a short putt, that little clubface manipulation becomes increasingly difficult to control. Don't make it harder than it has to be—line-up with your body and clubface square to the intended target line.

DRILL: String Putts

When you practice, take a piece of string with you and run it from the flagstick to a scoring pencil four or five feet away. Then practice putting straight putts under the string. A few minutes a day will improve your alignment. ■

FAULTS

9

CHAPTER

10

PRIVATE LESSONS

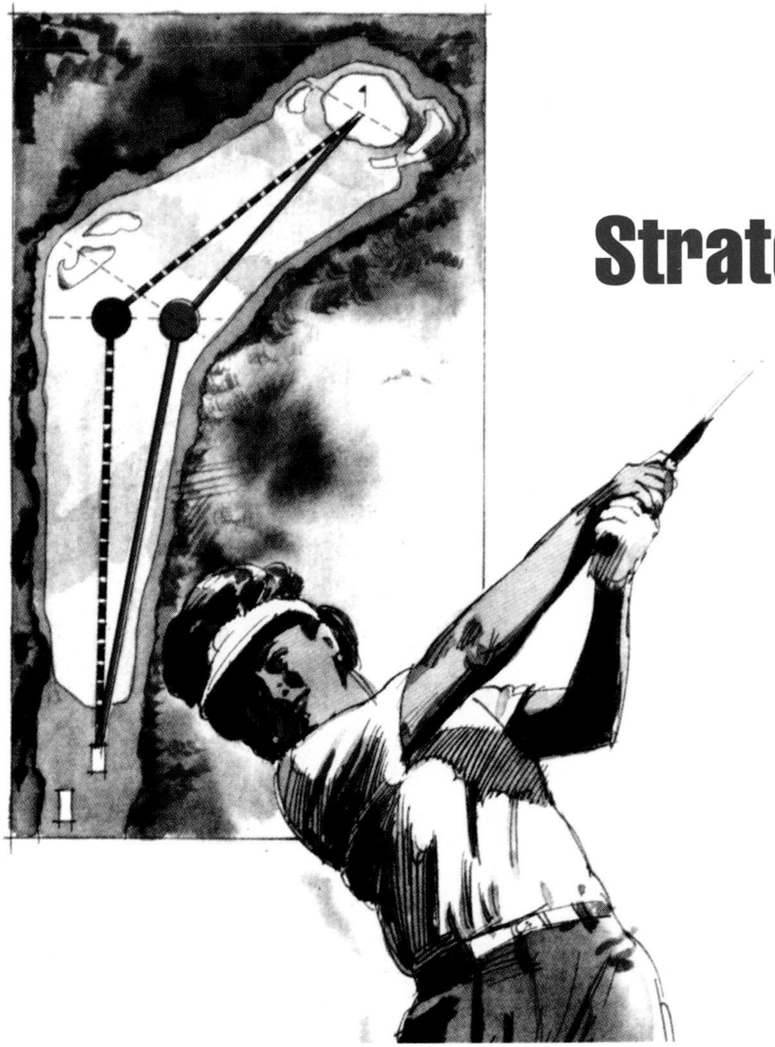

Strategy

PLAYING AGGRESSIVELY

PLAYING AWAY FROM THE PIN

PLAYING TO QUADRANTS

DEVELOPING ON-COURSE AWARENESS

UTILIZING THE LAY-UP

PLAYING AGGRESSIVELY

Do you fall into the rut of playing short, safe shots—always aiming for the middle of the fairway and green? You won't throw many shots away with that kind of strategy, but it's also a waste if you have the ability to hit precision drives and approaches. If you're looking to knock a few shots off your handicap, you may find that taking a more aggressive tack does the trick.

AIM FOR A SPOT, NOT JUST THE FAIRWAY

Long hitters can cut the corners of doglegs. If you lack the power to do the same, you can leave a much shorter approach by driving the ball close to the side on which the hole bends (so long as you hit it far enough to leave a clear shot at the green). The difference between putting the ball close to the corner and the middle of the fairway may be as much as 20 yards—two clubs. That translates into hitting the green in regulation and making par or coming up short and making bogey.

You will be left with a much shorter approach if you drive the ball close to the side in which the hole bends.

Your ability to put the ball where you want it should allow you to shoot for the pin— even near trouble.

GO FOR THE PIN!

The longer the approach shot, the more likely a player is to aim at the middle of the green instead of the pin. But if your shots are more unerring than the average player's, you don't have to play for the fat of the putting surface, even if you're hitting a fairway wood approach. Your ability to put the ball where you want it should allow you to shoot for the pin most of the time, whatever club is in your hand. That should hold true even if you have to bounce the ball short of the green close to a sand trap to roll it up next to the pin. If you do find trouble, your short game should be able to bail you out most of the time. You may play more chips and explosion shots, but you'll also end up facing many more short birdie putts. ■

STRATEGY

10

PLAYING AWAY FROM THE PIN

You're long and wrong and you know it. But playing aggressive golf suits your style and personality, so despite your wildness you still try to pull off risky shots. What really steams you, though, is when you try to do the smart thing—ignoring a sucker pin and aiming toward the safe part of the green—but you can't stop yourself from re-routing your clubhead path toward the flag during the downswing. The result is almost always trouble. How can you overcome this subconscious tendency to go for the stick, even when you consciously don't want to?

IMAGINE A SECOND GREEN

For the purposes of the "safe shot" you want to play, forget that the pin exists. But take it a step further. Don't only nix the pin, forget about that entire section of the green. Imagine that the putting surface has shrunk to the size of the area you're aiming at, no larger. If you prefer, picture a second pin on the "new" green, or pick out a secondary target in the background to represent it.

Secondary target

Imaginary pin and green

Imagine that the putting surface has shrunk down to the size of the target area.

Align feet, hips, and shoulders squarely to the "safe" target.

To help concentrate on swinging the clubhead toward your imaginary pin, take a half practice swing, stopping the follow-through so the club is parallel to the ground and pointing to the target.

SWING A CLUBHEAD TOWARD A SECOND TARGET

You may be resolved to aim away from the sucker pin and set up squarely toward safety, but it still doesn't always work out. Commonly, as you waggle into a comfortable position, you inadvertently shift your alignment back toward the real pin. So, make a point of planting your feet quickly and keeping them planted—no shuffling. Then, by aligning your hips and shoulders to the line of your feet, you can be sure you're aligned toward safety. But you aren't out of the woods yet. Even though your alignment is correct, it can be hard to resist trying to guide the ball toward the flag. To help prevent this, concentrate on swinging the clubhead straight toward your imaginary pin in your follow-through, not in the direction of the real flag. Take a practice swing next to the ball, aligning your body exactly as you want it, then make a half swing, stopping the follow-through so the club is parallel to the ground and pointing at your target. Focus on the feeling of passing through that point as you make your real swing. ■

STRATEGY

10

PLAYING TO QUADRANTS

Many players often describe their approach-shot strategy as "playing for the middle of the green" or "going for the pin." Neither option offers the best shot at low scores. Going for the pin leaves you vulnerable to sucker-pin placements and the hazards surrounding them. Playing for the middle of the green, although a safe alternative, may deprive you of a realistic chance at birdie, even if you hit a perfect shot. A better strategy is to divide the green into quadrants: front-left, front-right, back-left, and back-right. Depending upon the location of the pin, choose one quadrant as your target area. It's less risky than going for the pin but offers more scoring opportunities than playing to the middle of the green. Here's how quadrants work: The green is 60 feet deep and 60 feet wide, and the pin is in the back left corner. Choose the back-left quadrant. Now you've narrowed the target area to 30 by 30 feet, precise enough to make you concentrate but large enough to allow some margin for error. If the pin is in the middle of the quadrant—15 feet from the edges—the longest putt you'll face if you land in the quadrant is 15 feet. Hit the ball in the correct quadrant and you'll have a makable birdie putt.

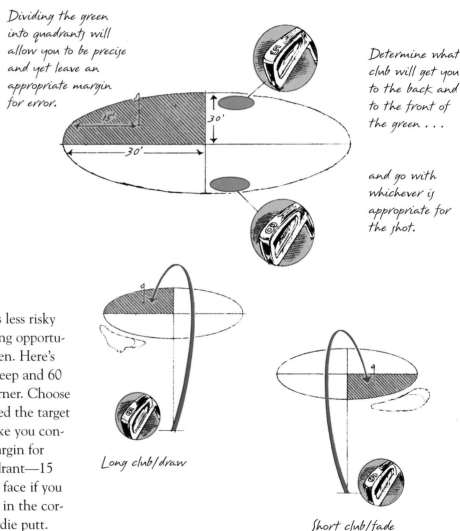

Dividing the green into quadrants will allow you to be precise and yet leave an appropriate margin for error.

30'

30'

15'

Determine what club will get you to the back and to the front of the green . . .

and go with whichever is appropriate for the shot.

Long club/draw

Short club/fade

DIALING IT IN

Club selection and shape of shot will help you dial into the necessary quadrant. Determine what club will get you to the front of the green and what club will get you to the back and go with whichever is appropriate for the shot. For a pin on the left side, aim toward the middle of the green and play a slight draw; for a pin on the right, play a slight fade. The right combination of short club/long club and draw/fade will send your ball to the correct quadrant.

SPECIAL SITUATIONS

Make no mistake, there are times when the smart shot is to play away from the pin. Don't change your thought process in these situations; just eliminate the pin from the equation. If the pin is cut behind a pond on the front left of the green and all you need is par to win your match, play for the front-right quadrant by hitting the shorter club and a fade. ■

There are times when the smart shot is to play away from the pin.

STRATEGY

10

DEVELOPING ON-COURSE AWARENESS

The difference between a truly satisfying round and one that's just so-so is on-course savvy. Being able to recognize and deal with the curves the course throws at you is your best shot at saving strokes. Here are two tips to keep in mind out there.

DIPS PLAY TRICKS

Every so often you have to ignore the yardage markers and let your eyes tell you what club to hit. When your instincts take over, be wary of dips or troughs in front of the green. Your eyes focus on a spot in front of the green to gauge distance, and if there's a section of ground unseen, it won't be factored into the equation. The same principle holds true for large bunkers in front of greens. If the lip is steep, it may appear that the green is directly behind the trap, even though there may be quite a bit of grass hidden from view. When estimating distance, account for all the ground between your ball and the pin.

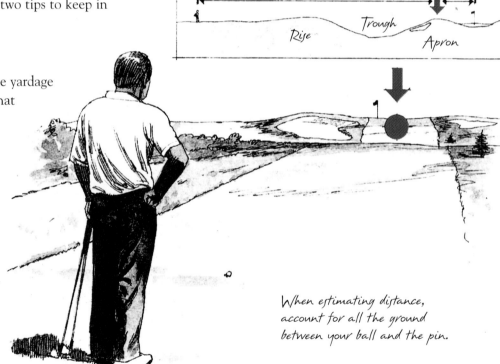

When estimating distance, account for all the ground between your ball and the pin.

BEWARE OF SHELTERING TREES

Ordinarily, you judge wind three ways: by feel, by tossing grass, and by checking the flag. Check the trees, too. Trees surrounding a hole block the wind, reducing its influence. If you can keep the ball low, under tree level, shots become easier; above the trees a wind-tunnel effect occurs and the breeze exerts a powerful influence on the shot. You also must be wary of holes with a tree-lined green or tee but with the rest of the hole exposed to the wind. Judge the wind in the exposed area, not in the trees. ■

Keeping the ball low will reduce the effect of the wind above.

Judge the wind by what's happening in the exposed area not in the trees.

UTILIZING THE LAY-UP

"Laying up" may be the least fun words in the game of golf. However, the lay-up shot plays a significant role in virtually every golfer's game plan. Remember: The inability to go for the green is not a sign of weakness. In fact, if you master the lay-up shot, it can become a powerful weapon.

REALLY LAY UP

You are 250 yards from the green of a par five fronted by a pond. The plan is to lay up short of the water for an easy approach shot. It would be nice if that shot was a flip sand wedge, but don't push too hard trying to get as close as possible to the water. The most important factor about the approach shot, regardless of the club you use, is that it is hit from a clean lie with a good angle at the pin, so you can be aggressive. If you're going to lay up, lay up. Don't flirt with disaster trying to get next to the pond. Leave plenty of room: You never know when the ball will hit a hard patch and take an extra bounce into the water.

BEAR DOWN

Amateurs often treat the lay-up like a wasted shot. Since the fairway is the usual target, the lay-up shot doesn't seem as precise as a real approach, so they

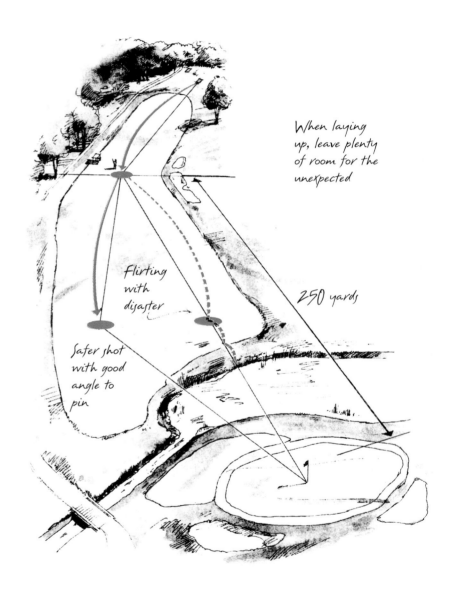

When laying up, leave plenty of room for the unexpected

Flirting with disaster

250 yards

Safer shot with good angle to pin

think you can hit it out there anywhere and be fine. Wrong! An errant lay-up usually costs more than an errant approach because it is vulnerable to more trouble. Don't be lackadaisical. Bear down and treat your lay-up with the same care you would an approach to an island green. The extra focus will carry over to your next shot, as well.

LOOK FOR LAY-UP OPPORTUNITIES

Lay-ups aren't limited to par fives. Sometimes, missing the green on a long approach can make your third shot, even if it's a chip or pitch, very difficult. Don't be afraid to lay up on long par fours, or even par threes, if the long shot seems particularly difficult. It may feel unnatural, but the payoff of lower scores will feel much better.

DRILL: Play Lay-Up

To sharpen your course management skills, play a round in which you lay up on every approach requiring a 5-iron or more. On each shot, pay close attention to identifying the optimal lay-up area for the next shot. Give yourself a small target and be meticulous about hitting it. ■

Be precise and treat your lay-up with the same care as approaching an island green

STRATEGY

10

Trouble Play

OVERCOMING THE EFFECTS OF CROSSWINDS

ANTICIPATING THE FLYER

TREATING YOUR WOODS LIKE IRONS

WORKING WITH LOW LIES

SAVING A SINKING ROUND

OVERCOMING THE EFFECTS OF CROSSWINDS

Good players compensate for a wind in their face or at their back by taking more or less club, respectively, the choice based on the strength of the wind and their experience. Crosswinds, however, affect direction rather than distance and prove troublesome even to the best players. Any crosswind over 10 miles an hour is likely to alter a shot's performance, particularly high, soft shots. In a strong wind, the smart strategy is to punch a three-quarter 7-iron rather than try to loft a 9-iron or wedge to the green. For longer shots, the choice is between riding the wind and fighting it. Here's how to master light and strong crosswinds.

LIGHT WIND: "HOLD" SHOT

You can cancel the effects of a light cross-wind—five to 10 mph—by working the ball into it: Hit a draw into a left-to-right breeze; hit a fade when it blows right-to-left. Aim straight at your target. That way, if the wind and ball flight cancel each other out, you'll be stiff. But if the wind picks up a bit or the ball curves slightly more or less than planned, you'll still finish close to your objective.

High, soft shots are more affected by crosswinds than low ones.

Aim directly at your target; regardless of the wind's strength the ball will end up near the target.

GOLF
MAGAZINE

Try to calculate how far the wind will move the ball, then pick a secondary target.

STRONG WIND: "RIDE" IT

When a heavy crosswind blows (more than 10 mph), you still should curve the ball against the breeze, while also allowing for the stronger gusts to move the ball their way. For example, counter a big right-to-left blow by aiming slightly left of the target and hitting a fade; the wind will bring it back. Only experience can tell you how far from the target to aim, but you can help yourself by aligning toward a secondary target off to the side. ■

TROUBLE PLAY

11

ANTICIPATING THE FLYER

You sometimes hear a pro complain about "catching a flyer" after an approach shot sails over the back of a green. A "flyer" is a shot that jumps off the clubface and flies much farther than expected. You can't do much to prevent a flyer, but you should recognize the conditions that might create one and plan accordingly. A flyer is caused by a foreign substance getting between the ball and clubface at impact. Blades of grass, from light rough or off a shaggy lie in the fairway, are the most common culprits. The grass covers the grooves on the club, reducing or even eliminating backspin. Backspin makes a shot rise; without it, the ball flies low and long. Wet conditions also can produce a flyer, especially with long irons. The sweeping swing path required to hit a long iron causes the clubface to pick up moisture from the grass as it approaches the ball. The water fills the grooves of the clubface, preventing them from doing their job. So watch for flyers out of wet rough or off a wet fairway. Not only does a flyer sail

Shot with backspin

Flyer

A flyer can be caused by blades of grass coming between the ball and club.

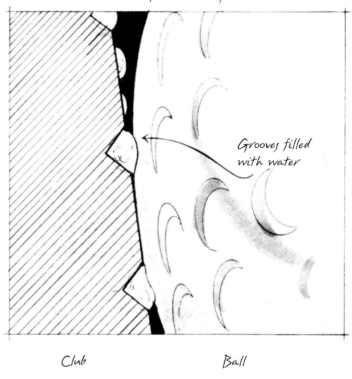

Wet conditions can also produce a flyer.

Grooves filled with water

Club   Ball

through the air, it continues rolling after landing. Again, the lack of backspin is the reason. With backspin, a ball bites and stops on a green; without it, the ball lands and keeps running. There's not much you can do when facing a flyer lie. But if a flyer looks likely, allow for it: Since you know the ball will fly lower, farther and land hot, you might take one less club on approach shots. You may even take two clubs less if trouble lurks behind the green. ■

TROUBLE PLAY

11

TREATING YOUR WOODS LIKE IRONS

No doubt you've heard that fairway woods are easier to hit than long irons. True. But to take advantage of the versatile 7- and 9-woods, recognize that these lofted clubs aren't just woods. In a sense, they're also irons and should be treated that way. Here are two examples.

ROUGH

The bigger, more rounded head of a utility wood is more effective than the blade of an iron at digging the ball out of rough. But that doesn't mean you can use the sweeping swing that works from a normal fairway lie and expect good results. To get the ball out, the club must approach the ball on a steeper path with a descending blow so it doesn't snag in the grass before impact. To do this, play the 7- or 9-wood much as you would a short iron. Position the ball in the middle of your stance, choke down on the grip about an inch and push your hands slightly ahead at address. Then, without letting too much weight transfer to the right side, take the club back on a steep path and hit down into the back of the ball. Keep your weight left to encourage a steeper path. The extra loft will shoot the ball up and out of the long grass.

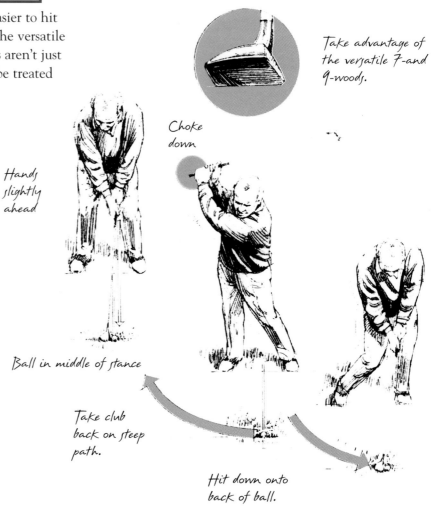

Take advantage of the versatile 7-and 9-woods.

Choke down

Hands slightly ahead

Ball in middle of stance

Take club back on steep path.

Hit down onto back of ball.

CHIPS FROM POOR LIES

If you mishit a chip with an iron, it usually means a long putt for your next shot.
With the more rounded sole of a fairway
wood, the chance of the club snagging in
the grass is greatly reduced. That's why a
7- or 9-wood makes sense when chipping
just off the green from a thick lie. Choke
down to the end of the grip, use a narrow,
open stance—so you can see the line of
your shot—and position the ball midway
between your feet. The swing should be a
sweeping action, like a putt. Even if you
make contact behind the ball, the sole
will still slide through the grass and provide plenty of force to pop the ball over
the apron so it lands on the green and
starts rolling toward the pin. ■

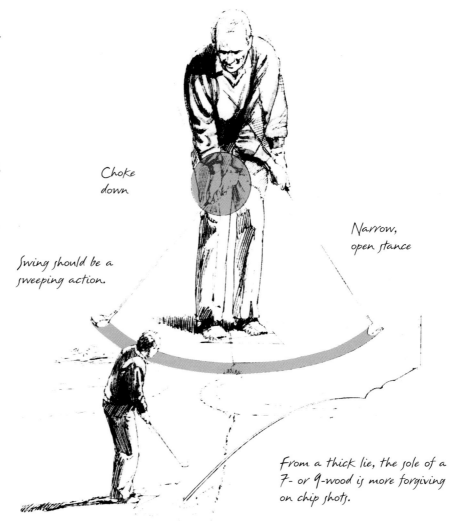

Choke down

Swing should be a sweeping action.

Narrow, open stance

From a thick lie, the sole of a 7- or 9-wood is more forgiving on chip shots.

TROUBLE PLAY

11

WORKING WITH LOW LIES

Have you ever looked down at your ball and not liked what you saw? Instead of sitting up nicely, the ball is down in the grass or a depression in the fairway. You get the feeling that solid contact is impossible, which creates a self-fulfilling prophecy. You must learn how to play a shot that's sitting down in thick grass, a low spot in the fairway, even a divot. What you don't want to do is force a normal swing through the lie, or worse, try to lift the ball out by swinging up. Either way, you'll probably hit behind the ball and advance it only a fraction of the necessary distance. Solid contact

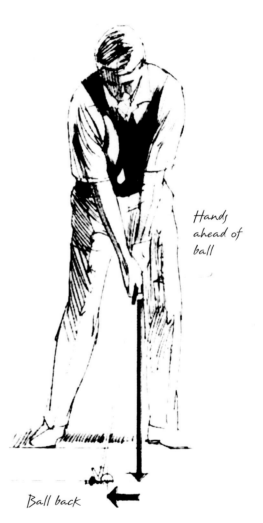

Hands ahead of ball

Ball back

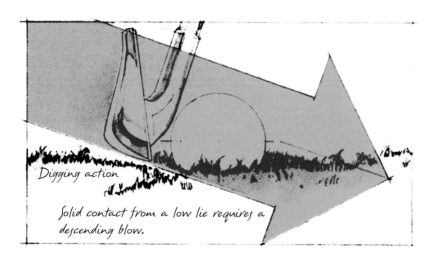

Digging action

Solid contact from a low lie requires a descending blow.

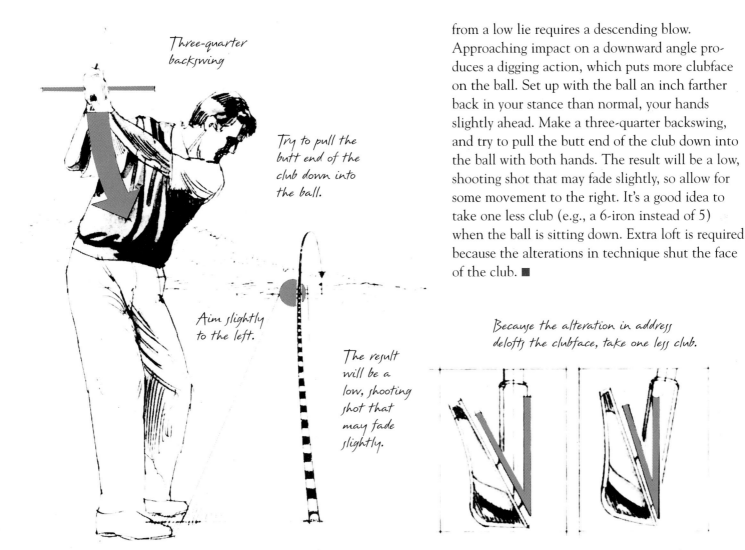

Three-quarter backswing

Try to pull the butt end of the club down into the ball.

Aim slightly to the left.

The result will be a low, shooting shot that may fade slightly.

Because the alteration in address delofts the clubface, take one less club.

from a low lie requires a descending blow. Approaching impact on a downward angle produces a digging action, which puts more clubface on the ball. Set up with the ball an inch farther back in your stance than normal, your hands slightly ahead. Make a three-quarter backswing, and try to pull the butt end of the club down into the ball with both hands. The result will be a low, shooting shot that may fade slightly, so allow for some movement to the right. It's a good idea to take one less club (e.g., a 6-iron instead of 5) when the ball is sitting down. Extra loft is required because the alterations in technique shut the face of the club. ■

SAVING A SINKING ROUND

No matter how good a player you are, there are days when you don't have your best stuff. Either you can't find the fairway with your driver, the sweetspot with your irons, or the hole with your putter. Maybe it's a combination of the three. Although this can lead to some high numbers, the better players find ways to buckle down and prevent a couple of bad holes from ruining a round. The key is often as simple as a tiny change in your swing or strategy that allows you to put a few good shots together and reverse the momentum. Here are three such changes to use when you need a reversal of fortune.

WILD DRIVER: PLAY A HARD FADE

The better player's bad day with the driver usually means a frustrating search for that smooth swing that combines distance and accuracy. When it isn't working, you'll get a lot out of skipping the search altogether and taking a rip at the ball. A hard fade allows you to do this. Aim down the left side of the fairway, make a full turn, then hit the ball hard with your right side. Be sure to hold on past impact with the last three fingers of your left hand. This will keep the clubface slightly open, producing a fade. This aggressive move at the ball will let you swing more instinctively, while the fade gives you some extra control and keeps the ball in play.

Hit the ball hard with your right side and hold on past impact with the last three fingers of the left hand.

Clubface slightly open

GOLF
MAGAZINE

SHODDY IRONS: MORE CLUB, MELLOW SWING

When your irons are off, each shot becomes an effort to recapture that elusive feeling you had during your last good round. Sometimes, no matter what you do, it never clicks. Rather than trying to recreate some past feeling, make solid contact your first priority. To this end, take one extra club and make a three-quarter swing on your approach shots. Swinging easier will give you more command of the clubhead and the ball, and the best chance to string together a series of solid shots.

PUTTING: BOUNCE IT OFF THE BACK

There are a million-and-one fix-its you can apply to your stroke when the putts aren't dropping. You can change your stance, grip, stroke, or even the putter itself. But, sometimes, what's most helpful is forgetting about how you're putting or what you're putting with and focus on the hole. Bad putting usually manifests itself in short putts—10 feet or less. When you seem to be missing a lot of these, change your goals. Instead of thinking "I have to make this putt," which implies making a good read and a perfect stroke, resolve to bang the ball off the back of the cup and in. The effect is twofold:

Take one extra club and make a three-quarter swing.

Focus on the hole, and bang the ball off the back of the cup.

First, you're liberated from thinking about the mechanics of your stroke; and second, you're forced to eliminate most of the break and play your putts inside the hole. Chances are good you'll make far more than you miss. ■

TROUBLE PLAY 11